debbietravis' paintedhouse

bedrooms

more than 40 inspiring projects for
your personal sanctuary

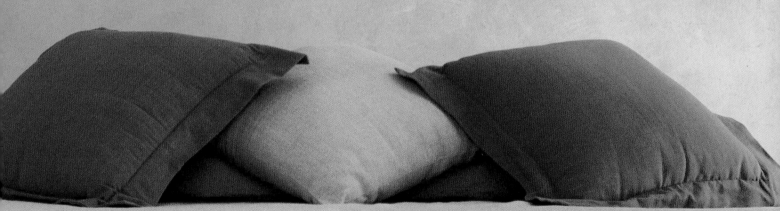

Debbie Travis with Barbara Dingle
Main Photography by George Ross

Clarkson Potter / Publishers
New York

Main photography copyright © 2002 by George
Ross. Step-by-step photography copyright © 2002
by Ernst Hellrung.

Published by Clarkson Potter/Publishers, New
York, New York. Member of the Crown Publishing
Group, a division of Random House, Inc.
www.randomhouse.com

CLARKSON N. POTTER is a trademark and
POTTER and colophon are registered trademarks
of Random House, Inc.

Printed in Japan

Design by Jan Derevjanik

Library of Congress Cataloging-in-Publication Data
Travis, Debbie. [Painted house bedrooms]
    Debbie Travis' painted house bedrooms /
Debbie Travis with Barbara Dingle.-- 1st pbk. ed.
        p. cm.
Includes index.

1. Bedrooms. 2. Interior decoration.
I. Dingle, Barbara. II. Title.
NK2117.B4 T73   2002
747.7'8--dc21   2002005387

ISBN 0-609-80548-7

10 9 8 7 6 5 4 3 2 1

First Edition

To Hans, with whom I share my bed and the most precious of memories.

acknowledgments

I owe an enormous debt to all the homeowners who generously allowed not only a photographer but also a whole television crew to invade their most private room. I'm grateful to all the photographers who captured the spirit of every bedroom for this book. This team includes George Ross who battled his way through snowstorms and heat waves from New York to meet me in the different locations. Only his cheery personality surpasses his great talent and stylish eye. Ernst Hellrung was responsible for the step-by-step pictures—he's great with a lens and a hammer. Cookie Kinkead had the lucky job of photographing hotels in the Caribbean and Miami, and my old friend Marcus Wilson Smith traveled the world in search of the perfect hotel. Thanks also to Gary R. Hall for the Lake Placid photography, Kim Christie for the photo on page 27, and Peter Sellar for Sheer Magic.

Once the pictures are taken, the writing begins. Barbara Dingle has an uncanny knack for climbing inside my head, rearranging all my thoughts, and then getting them down on paper. The job is long and demanding but she's always on top of it! Thanks, Barb. Big kisses and hugs also go to Dana MacKimmie, who painstakingly organizes every project in the book and keeps us all honoring our deadlines.

It is all the work behind the scenes that eventually gives us our inspirational rooms. My art directors are Alison Osborne and Anne Cote. Anne brings an enthusiasm to her designs that is passionate and unique. I must embrace my team of artists and painters who are not only incredibly talented but are all part of the Painted House family: Stephanie Robertson, Lynn Roulston, Hubert Simard, James Simon, Susan Pistawka, Yves Prud'homme and Allone Koffkinsky (Mr. K). My immense gratitude goes to Valorie Finnie and Elaine Miller, who style and dress each room with an individual freshness.

My editors Margot Schupf and Annetta Hanna are geniuses with a blue pencil. Thanks also to Marysarah Quinn and Jan Derevjanik, who make my books look as scrumptious as the best cooking books.

I would like to give a very special thanks to all the television networks around the world that air *The Painted House*. It is watched in many languages from the United States to South America, from Belgium to England and all the way from Canada to Australia. Finally, I would like to thank the viewers who let me into their homes every week. I wish I could give each of you an incredible bedroom makeover.

contents

preface   9

sweet dreams are made of this   10

elements of the bedroom   14
inspiration from afar   28
plan, prepare, and paint   44

bedroom makeovers   60

plantation bedroom   62

lattice border   64
four-poster bed   65
colonial floor   66

her sanctuary   68

dream canvas   70
sheer delight   72
fake fireplace logs   72
pencil stencil   74

putting on the glitz   76

gilded headboard   78
foiled bedside tables   80

gentlemen prefer flannel   82

suitable walls   84
blazer buttons tabs   85
pinstripe desktop   86
continental cushions   87
houndstooth dresser   87

radiant blue   88

midnight sky walls   90
rollered mural   91
paint underfoot   92
tufted headboard   94

sheer magic   96

platform bed   98
pop art   99
whimsical window frame   100

guardian angel   102

golden patina ceiling   104
shadow stripes   106
bed canopy   107
crackle table top   108

french country   110

provençal walls   112

gingham guest room   114

gingham walls   116
stenciled floor   118

grand opera 120

painted ceiling
  swag and tassels 122
faux wrought-iron
  headboard 125
veiled walls 127

wood and whimsy 128

burled wood
  cupboard doors 131
faux wood headboard 133

earthy origins 136

antiqued walls 138

italian style 140

painted panel walls 142
beamed ceiling 145
handmade headboard 145

something old,
something new 146

old door headboard 146

parisian boudoir 148

walls with a french twist 150
faux boiserie 151

all spruced up 152

cedar walls 154
corner detail 155
silvered shelf 156
grommet curtains 157

urban sleek 158

paneled wall 160

cottage bedroom 162

cottage shutters 164

ebony & ivory 166

ebony on a
  plywood budget 168
etched mirror 170

resources 172
index 174

preface

a place to dream

The bedroom is the most personal space in our home. This is where we begin each new day with renewed energy, ready to face the world. It's also where we end our day, tired but wrapped in the comfort of our familiar surroundings.

In my home the bedroom is the catalyst for some of my strongest family memories: lying in bed with a new baby, toddlers making the early-morning climb onto the bed, and teenagers sharing conversation and their many worries. We begin our birthday celebrations all crammed on the bed surrounded by wrapping paper, gifts from the grandparents, and cups of tea. This room is where I have read to my children, from their first simple stories to helping them appreciate the classics.

The bedroom should convey warmth and comfort. In my home any elements that distract from this, such as a work desk or even a television, are kept in another room. But we all have our own approaches, different space parameters, and varied budgets. I hope that you will discover a special setting, a new paint technique, or an inspirational furniture fix-up among the beautifully eclectic variety of bedrooms in this book. We all need a place to dream.

sweet dreams are made of this

We begin this book with a look at the elements that go into planning a bedroom. Each room becomes more than the sum of its parts, more than a bed to layer, or a window to lavish with swags of toile, or a dresser to paint. When completed successfully, the colors, fabrics, and furnishings speak to one another, and join together to accentuate a mood and carry a style.

The bed is the focal point and its main function is comfort. Buying the right mattress is crucial. There is much to learn about what kind of mattress is right for you, and how to mix this comfort with the style you like. The mattress is the first and most important building block of the bed.

You may already have a bed frame, a hand-me-down wooden headboard from your family, or a wonderful wrought-iron or brass bed. If you prefer, these can be reinvented to suit today's mood, and I have also offered many techniques for creating your own headboard.

You will need luscious layers of sheets, duvets, and blankets. In the first part of this book I'll share tips on what to look for and what questions to ask when shopping. Careful attention should be paid when choosing bed linens. Buy the best you can afford. Good-quality linens will last many years and numerous washes. They will envelop you in luxury and will save you money in the long run.

Storage for clothing is required, and places to put your bedside reading. Lighting is also important, whether it's the sunshine that welcomes in a new day or the ideal reading light.

Before you venture out to choose bedding, you must first decide what type of bedroom fits your personality and lifestyle. How will you use this room? Do you sleep alone? Do you work in bed, watch TV, or spend lazy Sundays pampering yourself? Does your partner share in the decorating decisions or does he or she leave it all up to you? Maybe you're designing a guest room, or your bedroom is part of an open loft. Once you have decided how the room is to be used, then think about the style. Is it to be a sexy room or have a sleek, contemporary design? Do you favor a room filled with natural light, or cocooned in a sultry candlelit space?

To help you get inspired, I have chosen some of my favorite hotel rooms from around the world. Whether it's a breezy oasis in Jamaica, or the rustic decoration of an Adirondack lodge, there is always something that we can borrow from these splendid venues and incorporate into our own homes.

Making over a bedroom, like any other room, takes planning and preparation. Walls need to be prepped before fresh paint goes on; renewing and reinventing furniture that you've had for years or just picked up at a flea market will require cleaning and sanding first. If you are pulling up wall-to-wall carpet, the floor will need attention. If the room lacks any architectural details, you may choose to add moldings. There is a huge variety of molding styles at your lumber store, primed and ready to put up and paint.

Being aware of what types of paint and other decorative materials are available for your decorating needs is half the battle. Knowing how to use them properly and to your advantage will guarantee a long-lasting result. So dig into the preparation section before you begin, or whenever we refer to it in individual project instructions. You will always save time and money in the end.

Once the mood and style of the room are decided upon, the different bedroom makeovers in this book will help you put your vision onto the walls, floors, and furnishings. Borrow a wall finish from one bedroom and a window treatment from another. Inject your own color sense into the project. Remember there are no hard-and-fast rules in decorating. Plan to please yourself.

elements of the bedroom

It has never been so easy to tailor a bedroom to your own tastes. Bedroom suites and wall-to-wall carpets have given way to a more relaxed combination of furnishings and floor coverings. Whether you are starting from scratch or planning a makeover, it's helpful to think about each of the components that contribute to the overall look and feel of the room. The bed and how you dress it is going to have the biggest impact on this private space. The bed is the largest piece of furniture, and in smaller bedrooms it will even take up most of the floor space. The other furniture—dressers, armoires, chairs, and bedside tables—as well as wall colors, floor finishes, and window treatments will all be chosen to complement the style and mood you set with your bed.

There is no end to the possibilities. Country themes will never lose their charm. Traditional chintzes, rich brocades, and velvets hold time-less classical elegance. Do you love the big bed look—a deep mattress raised high off the floor, covered with a lofty duvet and mountains of pillows? Or are you of a sleeker frame of mind—minimal height, per-haps a single mattress set onto a platform, with covers tucked in and simple, serviceable pillows? Whatever look you wish to achieve, there is an exciting range of beds, linens, fabrics, paint colors, and techniques to inspire you. Here's an overview of what you will need to make your dreams sweet and your spirit rested.

the bed

The style of the bed you choose plays a major role in the overall design scheme. You can spend thousands of dollars on custom brass, wrought-iron, or hand-carved wood bed frames. Case goods come at a more rea-sonable price. But you can also be innovative and hunt down marvelous flea market finds. When taking the secondhand route, be aware that antique bed frames were constructed for smaller mattresses, so you will have to make adjustments to allow for today's standard mattress sizes.

Old wood headboards may not have the design you are looking for, but with a little imagination they can be refinished with paint, stain, stencils, and paper to suit your taste.

If you love the idea of a brass bed, bear in mind that the beautiful rails and joinery will require a lot of rubbing to maintain their rich lus-ter. Brass can be bought clear-coated to save you the upkeep if you want the look without all that elbow grease.

Another design option for styling your bed is to design your own headboard. Create a unique headboard from fabric (page 78), an old door (page 146), medium-density fiberboard (MDF; page 145), or pieces of lum-ber (page 65). A contemporary concept is a platform built for the bed (page 98), which can include other components such as shelving and side tables. A single-size sleigh bed has its own traditional charm, and can double as a daybed/sofa set against the wall and dressed accordingly with lots of back pillows.

Four-poster beds were originally designed as frames from which to hang fabric canopies and side panels. These were required to keep out the cold and drafts in inclement climates, or to protect the sleeper from insects in the tropics. Modern building codes have eliminated these concerns, but the look is still popular. Swagging a bed with yards of fabric creates a luxurious and elegant mood and a sensual sense of privacy.

the mattress

You will spend one-third of your life lying on your mattress, so it's worth your time to investigate what's available and determine which construction and firmness is right for you. If you are sharing the bed with a partner, then both of your needs should be taken into account.

A coil-spring mattress will last longer with a box spring under it. The more springs in the mattress, the more comfortable it will be. Buy from a reputable store and ask the salesperson to assist you. The store may even have a mattress cut open to show you the inner construction. The coils should be made of a high-quality gauge and number about 315 coils for a standard bed. Layers of padding cover the top and bottom of the coils. The outer fabric is either cotton ticking or sateen with a high thread count for longevity.

Another variable is the firmness; a mattress that is too soft offers no support for your back and one that is too hard doesn't allow for the natural curves of your body. Either way, there's a good chance you will wake up aching, and the wrong mattress support can do long-term damage to your spine. How do you sleep: side, tummy, or back? Lie on the mattress in the store for a while and see how it feels to you. Once you have brought the mattress home, a good tip is to turn it around every six months. It should last ten to twenty years. A standard mattress measures about 8 inches high, as does the box spring. But there are now mattresses as deep as 17 inches, which are popular for creating that sumptuous "big bed" look.

Feather beds are the last word in luxury. Filled with down and feathers, they are made to lie on top of your regular mattress, offering the ultimate in gentle support and warmth. Fitted sheets are now available with deep gussets to accommodate the extra thickness of a feather bed or deep mattress.

A Japanese futon is a slim mattress traditionally made with layers of cotton, but now available with foam padding. The cotton will flatten down with use, and periodically requires a good beating to keep its shape. Futons are generally sold with a frame that can be folded into a couch or chair, depending on the size of the futon, as well as flattened out for sleeping. This versatile feature along with the relatively low cost make futons a popular choice for students and young people fitting out small apartments.

pillows

For sleeping, the proper pillow is a must to give your neck and spine the support they require. As a general rule, tummy sleepers need a flat pillow, back sleepers should choose medium support, and side sleepers need firm support under the neck giving way to medium support for the head. Pillows are stuffed with a variety of materials: foam and foam chips, polyester and poly-cotton blends, feathers, down and wool, and even buckwheat. A combination may also be used, such as wool clusters along with down to build up support where necessary. Down is softer, loftier, and more expensive than feathers. It's usual to find down mixed with feathers, but go for the most down you can afford for pure luxury. (See Allergy Control, page 20, for allergy concerns.)

For reading, writing, or watching TV in bed, you will want more substantial pillows to prop yourself up. These will also double as decorative accents, perhaps leaning against the headboard (or wall) when the bed is made. A large square pillow called a Eurosham or

Continental pillow measures about 26 inches by 26 inches. Complete the look with the size pillow that matches your mattress (standard, queen, or king).

Smaller pillow forms, 12-inch squares, round or oblong shapes, bolsters, and neck supporters are left to personal choice and style. These are essential if you are building a "big bed" look, want to display an eye-catching combination of patterns and textures, or are opting for an old-fashioned more is more, feathered nest.

bed sheets

Since the bed sheets (and pillowcases) are the material that touches your skin, it's important to get the best you can afford. The price is governed by three factors: the thread count, the type of fabric, and whether or not it is a designer product.

The main issue with sheets is the thread count. This refers to the

number of threads per inch. The more threads, the finer, softer, and more durable the sheet. The term *percale* designates that the product has a minimum of 180 thread count. Anything less is muslin, not very durable and quick to pill. A thread count of 200 to 210 is very satisfactory, and anything over 250 feels downright luxurious.

Poly-cotton blends are popular as they require no ironing and remain wrinkle-free on the bed. You will find plenty of variety in quality and design with these "wash and wear" sheets, but polyester does not breathe and consequently these sheets are not comfortable for warm sleepers. Also, they do not last as long as natural fibers. One hundred percent cotton is a natural product, as is linen. The price range can take quite a jump, but so does the quality. Egyptian cotton has longer fibers that make a softer, more durable sheet. An Egyptian cotton sheet with 200 thread count will feel like a regular cotton sheet with 300 thread count. Linen is spun from flax and is the most expensive sheet. It is more resilient than cotton, grows softer with each washing, and will last for years. It does, however, require ironing.

As with clothing, a designer label will bump up the price of bedding, and chances are good that you can find a similar color and thread count a few aisles over at a lower cost. Watch for sales—they are semiannual events at most stores, and you'll be able to upgrade with a clear conscience.

duvets and bedspreads

Visually, the style of the bed, the bedcover, and the presence or absence of a bed skirt and pillow shams define the style of the room. In master bedrooms, beds are growing—queen and king sizes are now the norm. This transfers to a large area to be covered. Therefore, the color and pattern of the bedcover will dominate.

Duvets are the most popular choice. The lightest, loftiest duvets are filled with a higher ratio of down to feathers. The duvet cover should have a high thread count to allow the down to breathe. Your body heat works along with the down to regulate a comfortable sleeping temperature. Any synthetics between you and the down, such as polyblend sheets or pajamas, will hinder the heat transfer.

Comforters made with cluster-fill polyester and cotton are suitable for those who like a lot of warmth when sleeping, and are less costly than down.

allergy control

With the amount of time spent in the bedroom, it is important to make the environment as healthy as possible. Unfortunately, allergies have become more and more common. There are many causes: dust, mold, mildew, pollens, synthetic fabrics, the detergents and softeners used to wash bedding, as well as chemicals found in decorating mediums such as paint, wallpaper glue, and carpets. There are products available that have been proven to help those who suffer from asthma or skin rashes. (See Resources, page 172.)

For the bed, there are mattress and pillow covers designed to seal out allergens (and also keep your mattress and pillows clean and fresh longer.) Buy 100% cotton or all-natural bed linens, launder in hot water and gentle soap, and avoid fabric softeners.

Until recently, down duvets have not been an option for allergy sufferers. But the down is now being processed in such a way that most allergens are removed. Look for *hypoallergenic* on the label, and talk to the salesperson about the success of their product, or any guarantees the manufacturer or store can provide. These duvets are worth the additional cost.

Foam pillows are available in numerous sizes and shapes. There are also pillows filled with buckwheat that are nonallergenic and give good support for the neck and spine.

Remove wall-to-wall carpets and opt for hardwood, cork, or other floor materials that do not give off toxic gases and are easier to keep clean. (See Floors, page 52.)

Water-based (latex and acrylic) paint is generally nontoxic, especially once dry, and it does dry quickly. If you or your child are very susceptible to allergies, there are also specialty paints available. (See Resources, page 172.)

Always check with a qualified medical practitioner first to identify the source of your allergy.

If your taste runs to damasks, velvets, brocades, or corduroy, which are heavy fabrics not really meant to be slept under, these make beautiful bedspreads or toppers that can be folded down at bedtime.

Handmade quilts, whether passed down through generations, discovered at a country fair, or store bought, will never go out of style. The history behind the intricate and colorful patterns along with the time and love that go into stitching each quilt make it a cherished part of the room's decor.

Chenille bedspreads are popular once again, as are soft Indian cotton and cotton pique, for those who like a lighter, pared-down bed.

blankets

Duvets are not for everyone. Being tucked under a cozy blanket or two is a familiar and comforting experience. Today there is a wide range of manmade blends along with the long-standing woolens that are easy-care and lighter weight. From the traditional Hudson's Bay blanket, perfect companion at the cottage or on the trail, to the tactile chenille and cashmere treasures that soothe the senses, the range of styles and prices and their versatile nature make blankets an exciting alternative.

storage strategies

There will never be enough closet space in a house or apartment. We are collectors by nature, and I find it impossible to locate a spare drawer or shelf anywhere in my home, especially in the bedroom. Storage is always a challenge, but there are ways to accommodate the overflow that are practical as well as good-looking.

Start with what you have, and if you live in an older apartment building or home, it will most likely be an undersized closet. A closet organizer will make all the difference, allowing you to use every square inch to advantage. If your bedroom has a large closet system, it should still be organized with a combination of hanging rods, shelving, and compartments for shoes, shirts, and sweaters. The rest of your storing you do with furniture pieces such as a dresser or an armoire, a blanket box or trunk, baskets, and boxes.

A well-made dresser can last many lifetimes; it probably will go out of style before it wears out. But a dresser is easy to transform with a lick of paint and a change of hardware. You can also add stock moldings and other decorative details to reinvent the piece. Reasonably priced case goods may fit your budget but not your style, so refinish these dressers the same way.

Armoires, originally produced to store clothing and bedding before built-in closets were thought of, have returned with increasing popularity. If your bedroom is a multipurpose space where you watch television, pay bills, or listen to music, an armoire also makes a great entertainment center for a TV, stereo, tapes, books, and files. Like the dresser, decorating it to enhance your decor is easy. Since armoires are quite large, one will be a central piece, along with your bed, for building a theme.

Blanket boxes and old steamer trunks are a good size to store linens or sweaters, and their flat tops make perfect places for piling up bedspreads and extra pillows while you sleep. They can also double as table surfaces.

Wicker baskets are invaluable for holding reading material, clothing accessories such as belts and handbags, photograph albums, and other memorabilia. They can be stacked or lined up on a closet shelf or slid under the bed for easy access. If you are going to store delicate items such as lingerie or sweaters in a wicker basket, make a fabric lining for the interior to prevent the wicker from snagging them.

Decorative boxes in graduated sizes are an attractive method for storing jewelry, correspondence paper and pens, and other miscellany. You'll find plenty of plain boxes in various shapes and sizes at the craft store. They can be embellished with specialty papers, decoupage, fabric, or paint, and make beautiful additions stacked on a dressing table.

other furniture

Bedrooms are also dressing rooms, and as such, require a mirror, full length if possible. This can be hung on the back of a door if space is tight. A boudoir chair and dressing table will give you a quiet place to prepare for the day, or night. If you have room, an upholstered chair

and footstool for reading or watching television adds another layer of comfort. Window seats mean a place to perch as well as extra storage built in underneath.

A bedside table is hard to live without. It holds the clock or clock radio, your book, a reading lamp, and favorite photos. Try to keep the articles on this table to a minimum. (But always find space for a tiny bouquet of flowers.)

It is not necessary that all the furniture in the bedroom match in style or age. But it helps to have a basic look in mind, and take cues from this to connect the pieces. It could be a specific color, or fabric, or a group of patterns that complement one another.

walls

When decorating the bedroom, if possible, choose bed linens and draperies first. They will be the major investment, and wall and floor coverings can then be selected to heighten the mood you have set. It's also far easier to take a fabric sample to the paint store than to struggle with shades of green or gray that you thought would complement the bedspread or curtains and be disappointed when you paint the walls.

The marvelous thing about paint (you may have heard me say this before) is that it can take on any personality. Paint can disguise, enhance, copy, dress up, and dress down. Your walls are the backdrop on which you can present a tranquil spirit with quiet shades of taupe, pale green, and earthy terra-cottas, or paint a fantasy of splendor by replicating marble slabs, stone pillars, and the look of lush fabrics. And this is a very budget-conscious versatility.

Although I'm not a terrific fan of wallpaper, I do love two types of specialty wallcoverings. Anaglypta is a heavy, embossed paper designed to be painted. Lincrusta is a much heavier linoleum-based wallcovering, also embossed with gorgeous patterns and meant to be painted. They are both available in the original patterns created a hundred years ago in

Britain. These products mimic the intricate detailing of carved plaster, and are perfect for creating a period style.

If you are living in a converted loft, one or more walls may be brick or concrete. The warmth of the brick tones can be picked up and painted onto other surfaces. Concrete is hard and cool. It can be painted, or you can play off its raw appearance with a minimal, Zen-approach sleeping space.

Cottage walls suit the natural quality of exposed wood beams and real wood paneling. If you want a lighter look, the wood can be white-washed, but its built-in warmth and personality make a wonderful escape from the concrete jungle.

ceilings

You might think more about the finish of the ceiling in your bedroom than in other rooms. It gets more visual attention as you lie back in bed, and its flaws will be more obvious. A few layers of paint will let you camouflage an uneven surface (see the golden patina ceiling on page 104). It's also worthwhile to apply special details with patterns and stencils (such as the swagged ceiling on page 122).

If you want to keep your ceiling clean and simple, paint it in a lighter tone of your wall color, and do the same for any moldings.

floors

Traditional wall-to-wall carpeting has given way to hardwood floors and area rugs. If you live in a new building that was carpeted by the builder, the floor will be a plywood subfloor rather than finished hardwood. As a stopgap until a new floor is laid, the plywood can be painted or stained and then varnished. It can replicate most types of floors—wood, marble, and metal—and you can even paint your own rug onto it.

Hardwood floors are beautiful on their own, but can also be enhanced with a pattern created with wood stain (see page 66.)

Sisal carpets play a big role in the natural bedroom along with 100% cottons or linens, simple unbleached curtains, and creamy white walls. Sisal comes in different grades and mixes. For a bedroom, where bare feet prevail, the wool blends are softer to walk on. It's possible to have a fabric border added to sisal carpets to bring attention to a special pattern already present in the room. (See page 25.)

Cork floors are another option. They are made from a renewable resource, are warm and forgiving underfoot, and come in a pleasing selection of designs. They are mid-priced, very tough and will last for years.

curtains and
window dressing

Although the trend today has moved away from heavy or fussy draperies at the windows, privacy is an issue in the bedroom. And there is also the matter of light to think about. Is it important for you to have a dark room to sleep? Blinds and shutters now come in a range of colors of metal, wood, and fabrics, and will block out both light and views. They can be fitted to sit inside the window frame for a neat, clean contemporary look.

Simple lined curtains will accomplish the same thing. Rather than yards of fabric and complicated drapery hardware, you can now get away with less width and use a rod pocket or loops to hang the curtains from a wooden or wrought-iron pole. Drapery panels are sold ready to hang and in some cases coordinate with bed linens. The no-sew generation has become very creative at avoiding all the hemming and stitching. Double-sided sewing tape for hems and seams, plus Velcro and the hot-glue gun for hanging, have revolutionized window dressing.

Fancy sheers such as metallic organza can be double-hung over a solid background as another simple way to make the room private and stylish. Sheers also come in an array of colors and patterns that make delicate, romantic window dressings. Hung from or draped over a rod, they can complete a room effortlessly.

Frameless windows can be decorated with paint to enhance the room's style and mood. A traditional approach is running a stenciled motif along the edges. I created a unique solution by painting a whimsical window frame that conveys the feeling of sheer fabric that continues across the wall (see page 101).

lighting

Illuminating the bedroom should revolve around how you use the space. If it is solely for romance and resting, then bring on mood lighting. Uplighting spreads light from the floor upward, bathing the walls in a soft glow that could filter through leafy plants or highlight photography and artwork. It is very soothing. Reading lights can have beams just large enough to focus on a book without disturbing your partner.

Task lighting is essential if you have a dressing table for applying makeup and doing your hair. A dresser or table lamp will boost the wattage when you are dressing, and, if put on a dimmer, can also become mood lighting.

Any of these elements can be the catalyst to decorating your bedroom. You may have a favorite bedcover, an old-fashioned bed, or an exquisite carpet. One of the wall techniques you have spotted in this book or a bolt of fabric you found on sale may fuel your imagination. Take the time to investigate the many exciting options available to you, and enjoy the process of pulling it all together.

inspiration from afar

The most difficult part of any decorating project is knowing where to begin. Whether we are working around our existing furnishings or starting from scratch, we all need a spark of imagination to get us enthused for the upcoming project. These ideas can come from any-where, but most of us rely on decorating books or magazines to give us an overview for our rooms.

Because they are such personal spaces, the concept and scheme of the bedroom should be looked at with different eyes than the rest of the house. This is the only room that is not on show to the world. Even with a house full of visitors, your bedroom door is closed, the room to be shared only with your loved ones. The luxury of designing a bedroom is the purely selfish thought of creating around your own needs. If you are planning a guest room, the sheer joy of decorating a relaxing envi-ronment for someone dear enough to stay in your home is special.

So where do you start? One of my favorite modes of gathering ideas and inspiration for a bedroom is through travel and viewing the remarkable boutique and specialized hotels that are now all over the world. For years we have longed for the comfort of home when we travel. Now the pendulum has swung back the other way and we are eager to re-create these hotel rooms in the privacy of our own homes.

Many of us have our first experience of sleeping on immaculate white linen sheets atop a feather mattress or surrounded by the delicate folds of mosquito netting when we are far from home. The delights of sleeping within walls washed in the boldest terra-cotta red or having shutters on the windows instead of traditional curtains all conspire to open up new possibilities for our own bedrooms. You may not live in a Mexican village or have the view from a Tuscan villa, but why not allow the impact of a memorable hotel room to influence the way you relax in your own bedroom?

Here are some of the unforgettable hotels that I have stayed in—rooms that have inspired me and The Painted House team to re-create their charm and uniqueness in ordinary homes.

island life

jake's, jamaica

Located in a small fishing village on the southern coast of Jamaica, Jake's is a truly unusual hotel. This secluded hideaway is a collection of individually decorated cottages painted in a series of Caribbean pastels. Sally Henzell is the owner and designer, and we became fast friends on my first visit. The eclectic mix of furnishings is the key to each bedroom's casual flavor. Sally has a decorating challenge very common to anyone living far away from a large city with its wide choice of fixtures, fittings, and furnishings, so she has used her vivid imagination to paint and furnish these rooms.

Sally has painted the walls in washes of earth colors, but these are not from the paint can. Sally uses the actual red Jamaican soil that surrounds the property. Diluted down, these natural tints are rubbed over the raw stucco in warm blended tones. She uses driftwood picked up from the nearby beach as shelving, molding, or door frames. Discarded bottles are pressed into the walls during construction to allow light to dance through the colored glass. Beads and shells embellish bed canopies and, of course, shutters, which allow in the sea breezes but keep out the scorching sun.

Sally has used the elements close at hand to create bedrooms that are both unique and intimate. You many not live on a Caribbean island, but the adventurous and eclectic simplicity of Jake's is a happy option for your own bedrooms.

italian opulence

palazzo terranova, umbria, italy

I was speechless when I first entered this truly stunning villa. Palazzo Terranova sits regally on the top of a hill in the heart of Umbria. But it was discovering that Sarah Townsend, the proprietor, was the imagination and talent behind the enormous renovation of this hotel that was most impressive. When I first spoke to her, transatlantic over a crackling phone line, she told me that Terranova was her Italian love story. It is the realization of one woman's dream to turn an ancient ruin into a glorious retreat for the discerning traveler.

Sarah has used the versatility of paint to bring back the charm of the original structure and to emulate the surrounding land. The color palette has been drawn from the earth colors and the vegetation, which changes with the seasons. The walls in each bedroom have been color-washed straight onto the rough plaster, sometimes in bold stripes or in flowing patterns to replicate the ambience of draped fabric.

This is the room I was lucky enough to stay in on my visit to Terranova. The beamed ceiling has been stenciled in authentic medieval designs, and the dado has been painted to look like marble panels. The bedrooms are sumptuously equipped with oversized wrought-iron beds, the best-quality linens, and a lovingly restored collection of antique furnishings.

Motivated by Sarah's enthusiasm for her home and hotel, we can also create grandeur and elegance with the inventive use of paint (see Grand Opera, page 120).

english charm

charlton house, somerset, england

If you dream of a bedroom filled with romantic fantasy, rooms designed around a bygone era, look no further than the stately homes of England. Charlton House is such a place. Situated in the rolling hills of Somerset in southern England, this magnificent hotel is owned and designed by Roger Saul. He is the man behind the Mulberry Collection of leather goods, fine fabrics and furnishings. His truly British taste has been incorporated into every guest room. Each bedroom evokes a way of life from the Elizabethan period. Grand antique four-poster beds, romantic lighting, and deeply textured fabrics are the ingredients of a royal bedroom. The walls in old homes are made from lathe and plaster. The traditional way to paint these old surfaces is to "wash" the walls with tinted limestone. This creates a layered effect of chalky color. The finish is hugely popular today because it gives character to our modern, sterile drywall. Limestone is extremely toxic, but latex paint thinned down with glazing liquid is a good alternative when washed over the wall. Although Charlton House is set deep in the British countryside, the English style that it emulates is one of the most sought after decorating styles in the world.

peace of mind

the W hotel, new york city, new york, u.s.a.

I visited The W Hotel in New York during a hectic business trip. It was a perfect choice for a busy few days. As you walk into the lobby from the frenzy and noise of Lexington Avenue, you are greeted with a mood that is set to soothe the senses. There are gigantic windows of stained glass, a serene wall of water, and groomed pots of wheatgrass. But it is the bedrooms that bring your heart rate tumbling back to normal. They have been designed not only for comfort, but as a cocoon to help you recharge your batteries. The color palettes are soft beiges, sage greens, and white. The walls are stenciled in floating leaves with a touch of gold. You snuggle into a deep down duvet and sheets printed with soothing phrases such as "sing with spirit," "sleep with angels," "dance with abandon," and "love with compassion."

If you wish for a bedroom that is tranquil, a place to close the door and catch your breath, then take a tip from The W Hotel. You don't need a large room, or fancy furnishings, just a good-quality mattress, crisp white sheets, and a tray of calming wheatgrass.

And by the way, if you are curious as I was about the meaning behind the hotel's name, W stands for "warm, welcoming, wonderful, wonder why no one ever did it before."

south beach style

the kent, miami, florida, u.s.a.

If your taste in the bedroom is bold, then look no further than Miami's famed South Beach. Here you will discover a collection of intimate hotels that replicate this eclectic area. The Island Outpost properties are each theatrically designed around different themes. Although each one has its own personality, they are all exciting experiences to visit. The Kent, a restored Art Deco hotel, has been updated to reflect the youth and buzz of life of the surrounding area. Brightly colored bedding coordinates with the clean lines of the furnishings and honey-colored woods. For a cheerful statement in your bedroom or guest room, be inspired by the heat of Miami. You don't need a big budget, just paint in the most vibrant of colors.

adirondack style

lake placid lodge, lake placid, new york, u.s.a.

If you are looking for a rustic, homey bedroom, then a visit to the Adirondacks in northern New York State will transfix you with this distinct country style. The Lake Placid Lodge is a hotel in love with luxury, both personal and rustic. It is also the epitome of Adirondack style. The lodgings are filled with twig and birch-bark furniture, stone fireplaces, and the richly colored designs of Navajo fabrics. This hand-crafted wood furniture is now so immensely popular, it's available around the world. But it was the American pioneers who settled in the rugged north who first made their furnishings from the raw materials found in the nearby woods. The charm of today's Adirondack furniture is that it is still crafted in the same way.

The Lake Placid Lodge is a home away from home. It's a perfect place to curl up with a good book and a steaming mug of hot chocolate after a day of climbing or fishing. Its style combines incredible comfort with a sumptuous country flavor. Most of us do not have a fireplace in our bedroom, but wood-paneled walls, moldings, and trim painted to represent birch bark (you can also buy dried bark to cover furnishings), and deeply colored fabrics will wrap you in splendid solitude.

old world tranquility and elegance

hotel place d'armes, montreal, quebec, canada

The boutique-hotel revolution has been with us for a few years now, and I'm grateful for its place in design history. A boutique-hotel concept is designed around intimacy and the latest in chic style. These hotels are all unique in their design elements, from thoroughly modern to pure luxury. They are geared to personal comfort for the stylish traveler. Boutique hotels are popping up in every city and offer us many inventive ideas that we can use in our own homes. Hotel Place d'Armes is located in the area of Montreal known as Vieux Montreal. The Old World elegance of the exterior reflects the charm of the area and is seamlessly continued inside. A sense of tranquility is created by the soothing monochromatic color palette of soft neutrals applied throughout. This is balanced with tactile elements of deep cherry wood furnishings, the finest linens, and chenille throws. The oversized piece of molding placed above the bed is a simple way of adding decorative shelving. All these ideas can be re-created simply in your own bedroom. This is a room for cocooning, ideal for both the weary traveler and the homeowner at the end of a long day.

plan, prepare, and paint

I find that embarking on any new project is exciting and energizing. The idea of a fresh start, a new color on the walls, the thrill of transforming tired or dated furnishings into something not only serviceable but stunning, these thoughts drive me on. And whether it's for *The Painted House* television shows or for my own home, I have learned that proper preparation is the key to the success of any makeover.

The first step is the planning stage. I hope that the previous chapters and the imaginative makeovers in the second half of the book will help you focus on a specific look that's right for you. Once you know what you want to accomplish, then put the different tasks in order and allow enough time to accomplish each step. Make alternate arrangements for sleeping so that you can close the door on the space while you are working. Set aside one weekend for the preparation steps and then paint the next weekend when you are fresh and full of energy. Refinished floors require five to ten days to cure properly, depending on the heat and humidity, before you move furniture back in.

It may sound simplistic, but a well-planned makeover might mean the difference between finishing happy or literally sleeping in the doghouse! Here's the plan that works for me.

balance the budget

In any bedroom, if you are starting from scratch, the biggest part of your budget is going to be allocated to the bedding. Since the bed is the focal point of your room, buy the duvet cover, bedspread, pillow shams, and whatever else is seen on the bed first, and design the rest of the room around that. A good mattress, duvet, and bed linens can add up to a sizable amount, but it's money well spent, and you can save handily in other areas.

Be an educated shopper. Read the section on sheets, duvets, and bedspreads on pages 18 to 19. Quality sheets look better, feel better, and last longer, so they are a good buy. And there are semiannual sales in most department and specialty stores. Discontinued lines will be sold at a discount, as will "bed in a bag" packages, which combine matching sheets, pillowcases, and comforter. Remember to check the thread count.

Furnishings such as bedside tables, a headboard, a dresser, or an armoire can be salvaged from family and flea market, or bought economically and refurbished. This is where your imagination and a bit of paint pay big dividends.

Window coverings may be understated, but are necessary for privacy and to block out the light. There are simple solutions such as blinds and tab-top curtains made from sheers or sheeting that will complement your room at reasonable prices.

Paint is the most economical decorating tool there is, and as you will discover throughout this book, its versatility offers remarkable results for any style. So don't be disheartened if you have little money left over after you have shopped for linens. Paint is where you will save —it just won't look like it.

Always buy the best-quality paint. The colors will be truer, it goes on more smoothly, and fewer coats are required to get good coverage.

materials and tools

Along with the step-by-step instructions for each of the room makeovers there is a list of the materials and tools required to complete the project. Here is a description of the products you will see. Unless otherwise stated, they are all available at paint and hardware stores or art and crafts stores.

latex paint is water-based, low odor, and quick drying. It is colored at the paint store using universal colorants, or you can tint it yourself with artist's acrylic paint or powders. Cleanup is with soap and water.

acrylic paint is also water-based, but has a higher percentage of acrylic resins than latex, and is very durable. It is colored the same way as latex paint. The properties of latex and acrylic paint are different, and they do not mix successfully. Cleanup is with soap and water.

oil (alkyd) paint is oil-based, has a strong odor, and takes up to 24 hours to dry. It is colored in the paint store with universal tints or you can tint it yourself with artist's oils or powders. Because it has a longer open time, it used to be the only option for creating paint effects, but good-quality water-based glazing liquids have solved this problem. Cleanup is with paint thinner.

artist's acrylics are sold in tubes, have the consistency of toothpaste, and are water-based. They are used to tint water-based paint or glaze. Their pure colors add authenticity to paint effects such as marble. Cleanup is with soap and water.

artist's oils are sold in tubes and can be used to tint oil-based paint and glaze. They are toxic. Cleanup is with paint thinner.

powders are used by professionals to color any type of paint, glaze, or varnish. The color is very concentrated, so you do not need much. They come in metallic colors and can be mixed with regular paint to get a metallic glow. You must always wear a mask when mixing powders because they are toxic.

water-based glazing liquid has a milky color, but dries clear. It is mixed with water-based paints (latex and acrylic) to form a colored glaze.

colored glaze has two purposes: It makes the opaque paint translucent, so that you can see the base coat shining through it. Also, glaze has retardants in it that slow down the drying time, which allows you to manipulate the paint as directed in the instructions for paint effects.

Recipes for mixing colored glazes are given in the instructions. The more glaze to paint, the more translucent the colored glaze will be, and the longer it will take to dry. If you want a more opaque mix, add more paint. Cleanup is with soap and water.

oil-based glazing liquid has the color and consistency of white gelatin, but dries clear. It is mixed with oil-based paints. An oil-based colored glaze is recommended only when a very long open time is required, such as for creating certain kinds of marble effects, or if you are glazing over an oil base. Cleanup is with paint thinner.

wood stain comes water- or oil-based and in a good selection of colors. Along with the traditional mahogany, oak, pine, and other natural wood tones, there is now a range of pastel shades and deep colors. Whereas paint forms an opaque coat that sits on top of wood, stain sinks into the wood's grain and binds with the fibers, making a very durable finish. When staining raw wood it is important to sand the surface to open the wood's pores so that it will take the stain evenly. The only way to remove stain is to sand down to the depth into which it has soaked.

varnish is found under many names—urethane, polyurethane, clear coat, or top coat. For clarity's sake I have used the term *varnish* throughout this book. Adding a coat of varnish has two distinct purposes. First, it protects the painted surface from wear; second, it adds sheen to the painted effect. Varnish, like paint, comes in several sheens from matte to high gloss.

water-based (acrylic) varnish is a milky color in the can, but dries clear. It is low odor and quick drying. Unlike oil-based varnishes, it does not yellow, which makes all the difference to the colors it covers.

oil-based varnish must be used over oil-based paint, so take the yellowing into consideration if this is the case.

spray varnish must be used if you are protecting a finish that has been created with pencil, chalk, or any material that would rub off if brushed. Take the necessary precautions when using any spray product: Always wear a face mask, cover anything you don't want sprayed, and work in a well-ventilated area.

standard paintbrushes come in a variety of sizes from 1″ to 8″ wide. Synthetic bristles are best for latex paint, animal hair for oil-based paint. The tip of the brush is designed for different purposes. Angled tips are for cutting in around the edges of walls and trim. A tapered tip is also good for edging. A flat tip is used for general painting.

dragging brushes have long (4″ or 5″), very thick bristles, usually of horsehair, that leave distinct lines when pulled through a layer of wet paint.

badger-hair softening brushes are important tools for many paint effects, especially marbling. They are held perpendicular to the surface and brushed back and forth very softly, tickling the surface to soften and blend lines. They are expensive. An alternative is any soft-bristle brush such as a makeup brush.

stippling brushes are square or brick-shaped, flat-ended brushes with medium-coarse bristles. The handle is set at right angles to the brush and rotates. They are expensive. An alternative is any wide-bristle brush.

varnishing brushes are long-haired natural-bristle brushes designed not to leave brush marks. A good alternative is a sponge brush or sponge roller.

artist's brushes come in many sizes from 2″ down to just a few bristles for fine work. Price varies according to the quality of the bristles, sable being the most expensive.

stencil brushes are available in a variety of sizes from ⅛″ to 2″. The brush is flat-ended, and used for stippling or swirling the paint onto a stencil. Always use one brush for each color, and use a dry brush to apply the paint in very thin coats. You can use other tools to fill in stencils—sponges, foam brushes, rollers, and spray stencil kits (see stenciled floor on page 118.)

combing tools come in rubber or metal. The rubber is generally triangular, offering three tooth and spacing alternatives. The metal comb's teeth are longer and are used to create faux woodgraining.

sponges may be sea sponges, which have an irregular shape and large and small holes throughout, or the common kitchen sponge, which is rectangular and has much finer holes. Sponges can be torn or cut to get the size required for the job. Always wet a sponge first and then squeeze it out before dipping it into paint.

rags are used to create an imprint in the glaze. They must be soft, clean, and lint-free. Old T-shirts are the best.

rollers come in a variety of sizes and pile thicknesses. Low pile is used for latex paint, thicker pile for oil paint. There are specialty rollers for painting over stucco, as well as rollers that have a design cut into them. A thin roller head with a long handle is designed to fit behind radiators. Larger roller handles are designed to have an extension pole screwed into the end for reaching ceilings and high walls. Sponge rollers are good for applying varnish or latex paint and glazes.

paint trays are available in various sizes to correspond with roller widths. There is a trough for paint and a ribbed slope to facilitate even distribution of paint on the roller or paintbrush. The larger paint trays have U-shaped legs that can be hooked to paint ladders.

gold and silver leaf are traditionally used as lustrous accents for frames and decorative accessories and as opulent additions to walls and ceilings. Leaf is very thin and fragile, and applying it well takes practice and patience. Real leaf is very expensive; most leaf used today is imitation. The leaf is laid over a tacky sized surface, then brushed with a soft brush to adhere. Once dry, the residue is brushed away, leaving a smooth, glowing surface. Now available in many different colors.

metallic transfer foil is available by the roll or in sheets. It is designed to be transferred onto a flat surface. First size is applied to the surface and left to get tacky. The foil is laid onto the surface with the metallic side facing out, then burnished with a blunt tool. When the foil is peeled away, a metal veneer is left behind. These foils are not as luminous as their leaf cousins, but they are less expensive and an excellent alternative for larger jobs.

s i z e is a specialized glue used to adhere metallic leaf and foils to a surface. The size is brushed onto the surface; when it has dried to the tacky stage, it is ready to accept the leaf or foil. Dry size is now available and is rubbed onto the surface from transfer paper. (See Resources, page 172.)

a q u a s i z e is a water-based adhesive that goes on milky white and dries clear. When it is clear, but still tacky, leaf or foil is applied.

prepare the room

When the shopping is done and you're ready to go, clear as much out of the room as possible so it's safer and easier to work. You will be moving a ladder around and using extension poles to reach the ceiling and the tops of the walls. The less there is to bump into or trip over, the better.

Use painter's drop cloths to cover what can't be moved. Paint will seep through newspaper, and plastic is slippery and could cause an accident.

For the best results, it's important to prepare your surfaces properly before you start to paint so that the paint will adhere and your work will last.

walls

If walls have been previously painted, sand away any loose paint and dried paint drips, wash with a damp sponge, and let dry. Brush any loose material from cracks and holes, fill with spackle, and let dry. Sand repaired areas smooth. If the crack or hole is deep, apply two or more thin coats and let dry between coats. This will make a cleaner repair that won't split or pull away from the wall.

To remove wallpaper, begin with a commercial wallpaper remover gel. Wet the paper with a sponge, make long slits through the paper with the edge of a spatula, and apply the gel. Wait 10 to 15 minutes and then use the spatula to scrape off the paper. Don't dig or scrape too hard or you will scar the wall surface; it is better to repeat the process if necessary. For tough jobs, commercial steamers will speed the process along. Wear rubber gloves and take care, as both the steamer and the water get very hot. Once the paper is off, wash the walls to get rid of any bits of paper and glue. Let dry and repair as for previously painted walls.

priming

If the old paint is latex and it is a light color, there is no need to apply a primer. If you are not sure whether it's latex or oil, then apply an oil-based primer. You can apply latex paint over an oil-based primer, but you cannot apply latex paint over oil paint.

Note: If you live in a home that is more than 25 years old, the paint may contain lead. Sanding off lead paint is dangerous because the lead dust becomes airborne. Wearing a mask when working, scrape any loose or chipped paint, sweep up the particles, and dispose of them as your area designates for toxic materials. Wipe the walls with a damp sponge, let dry, and then apply an oil-based primer.

If the walls have previously been painted with a semi- or high-gloss sheen, sand to rough up the surface, and use a high-adhesion primer to give the surface the tooth required for paint to adhere.

Freshly plastered walls and new drywall must be primed first.

If your base coat is a dark color, have the paint store tint the primer. Darkening the prime coat will reduce the number of base coats needed.

ceilings

Always wear eye protection when working on the ceiling.

Prepare the ceiling as you would the walls: Clean, fill any cracks, and prime any dark-colored ceiling or fresh plaster, including repairs. Ceiling paint is a flat or matte white and has a chalky texture. It is less expensive than regular paint, but is far less durable and not meant to be cleaned. Ceiling paint doesn't take dark tints very successfully. If you are going to paint a dark color or apply a paint finish to the ceiling, then prime with a water-based primer and use regular paint. Never use ceiling paint on walls.

The stucco ceilings common to new buildings are a challenge. Even cleaning with a damp cloth can pull away the pointy bits. However, it's quite a job to scrape and sand the ceiling smooth. You must use an oil-based primer over this type of stucco. A water-based primer will soak into the stucco and cause it to pull away from the ceiling, making quite a mess.

floors

Wood floors can be prepared either at the beginning or the end of the room makeover. If you are going to sand the floor, it is best to do this first. Either have it sanded professionally or rent an industrial sander to do it yourself. Be careful not to gouge the wood; it takes a light touch. Let the dust settle overnight and clean the walls and the floor.

If you have removed wall-to-wall carpet, there will be numerous nail and staple holes. Sand the floor first to get rid of any old varnish, paint, wax, and ground-in dirt. If holes are still noticeable, repair with wood filler.

Cover the floor completely with heavy-duty painter's drop cloths before you paint the ceiling or walls as any paint drips will soak into the raw wood floor.

furniture

Before embarking on a furniture fix-up, examine the piece for structural problems that cannot be solved with a coat of paint, such as large cracks, wobbly legs, drawers that stick, and warping. Hardware can be replaced and the surface renewed, but the piece should otherwise be in good condition.

With the availability of today's high-adhesion primers, it is no longer necessary to strip old wood furniture down to the raw wood before repainting. Sand away any chipped or loose paint, as well as paint drips or bumps. Sand to rough up a shiny surface, and wipe away the dust with a tack cloth. Apply a coat of high-adhesion primer and you are ready to paint.

If you do want to get down to the raw wood, use a commercial paint and varnish stripper. Always wear heavy-duty gloves and a mask, and work in a well-ventilated area as the chemicals in the stripper are toxic. Brush the gel-like stripper onto the surface, leave for the time recommended by the manufacturer, and then use a spatula to remove the finish. In areas that have many coats of paint, you will have to repeat the process. For hard-to-get-at crevices and joints, use steel wool that has been dipped into the stripper gel. Once all the old finish has been removed, wash to clean any residue left behind and let dry. Sand smooth, and use wood filler to make any small repairs.

If you are going to stain the piece, sand all the wood to open the pores so that the stain can soak in.

Furniture made from laminates or metal can also be refurbished with paint. Clean the surface well, then sand to rough up the surface. Remove any rust from metal. Apply the appropriate primer, either high-adhesion or metal primer, and then you are ready to paint.

adding architectural details

There are many ways to apply architectural interest to walls and furniture. Strips of molding can be added directly onto a wall to make panels (see Urban Sleek, page 158). Stock molding dresses up an old door to create an enchanting headboard in Something Old, Something New, page 146. Architectural depth can also be given to a wall by extending a small baseboard with varying widths of paint.

Depending on the style you are building, you may want to add some traditional architectural moldings to your bedroom, or enhance details that are already in place. There is a wide variety of moldings and trims at lumber and hardware stores that come in wood, MDF (medium-density fiberboard), foam, and (more expensive) plaster and are meant to be painted. There is also custom-made quality wood that is meant to be stained or simply varnished so that the grain can be seen. All moldings and trim work are generally sold in 8-foot lengths.

Crown or cornice molding is applied around the ceiling. You may select one or more designs and build a deep cornice depending on the height of the walls. For a 9-foot wall, a 4- to 6-inch depth is adequate.

Baseboards run around the wall at floor level. The minimal 3-inch strips that are found in most new buildings can be built up to a more substantial height of 5 to 8 inches.

Trim framing windows and doors, usually about 4 inches wide, can be enhanced by inserting square ornaments at the corners. This not only looks good, but it also saves you from having to miter the corners of the trim.

trim for furniture and headboards

You can reinvent the look of any piece of furniture. Build it up with pieces of wood or MDF cut to suit, such as we did for the old door headboard on page 146. Add strips of border molding to enhance the flat face of a dresser, table, or armoire. Paint will bring uniformity to the surface so that you will not be able to tell the old from the new.

Decorative techniques and materials can also transform a piece. Apply metallic leaf to a tabletop (page 80), or decoupage a bedside table (page 109). Trompe l'oeil effects such as the pinstripe desk on page 86, the tufted headboard on page 94, and the burled cupboard doors on page 131 create the rich feeling of fabric or fine wood at little cost.

measuring and marking

Whether it's for a ceiling border, stripes or panels on the wall, or a pattern on the floor, measuring and marking out your guidelines is an important part of the preparation. There are tools that make it an easy task.

retractable measuring tapes pull out from 6 to 9 or 10 feet, and are useful for measuring large spaces such as the dimensions of your room. There is a metal lip on the end of the tape that can be hooked around or pressed into a corner, and the metal is flexible so that it will bend when required. There is also a locking device so that you can hold the measuring tape at a specific measurement—handy for marking off stripes or any other repeat.

metal rulers and right-angle rulers give firm support for marking off straight lines. The angled ruler makes quick work of marking out a grid.

a level is a metal or plastic straightedge with one or two small containers of liquid set into it. The level of the liquid will tell you when your vertical or horizontal line is straight.

a plumb line is a piece of string with a hook on one end and a weight on the other. You can make one yourself. It is used to check for true vertical. Hook or tape the top to the wall and let the string hang free. The weight (and gravity) forces the string to hang perfectly vertically. Tape a plumb line into position and use a metal ruler to draw in the line. This is particularly useful if you don't have a level.

a chalk line is a piece of string rolled inside a container filled with chalk dust. When the string is pulled out, it is covered with chalk. It's used to mark a straight line between two points, and is easiest to manage with two people. If you are on your own, you can tape one end down and walk the line to the other point. Hold the string taut and ping it against the surface, leaving a straight chalk line behind. Chalk lines can be used as plumb lines.

If you are planning to repeat a pattern around the room, it is best to start from the center of the wall and move outward to the corners. This way, any incomplete design will be even on both sides, and the design will look symmetrical. If you want to have only completed designs, mark off a border to fill out the space.

Use what's already there to line up grids, rectangles, squares, and borders. For example, the boards in a wood floor offer straight lines to run a border, and a parquet floor is already set in a grid pattern.

When marking a border around the top of a wall, measure down from the ceiling. Our eyes naturally line up the two closest parallel lines. Similarly, when marking off a dado or chair rail, measure up from the floor, usually about 3 to 4 feet.

taping

The tape that I use for all my marking is low-tack painter's tape. It is made specifically to protect areas you don't want painted, and can be removed without causing damage to the underlying surface. Masking tape is so sticky that it will pull away surface paint and even plaster when you remove it. Low-tack painter's tape comes in a variety of widths, which makes it perfect for marking off grout lines around stone or tile and for creating different-sized stripes.

Apply painter's tape over a dry surface. If you have just painted the surface, allow it to dry for at least 4 hours before taping. Overnight is safest. Press down firmly along the edge against which you are going to paint. Remove the tape as soon as you have finished your work, pulling it back slowly.

If you have a stucco ceiling or the line between the ceiling and the walls is uneven, measure about $\frac{1}{2}$ inch down from the ceiling and tape along this line. Paint the ceiling color down to this line and you'll have a nice neat edge.

You will see in the project instructions that I recommend taping off a wall at the corner when doing a paint technique. This will give you neat corners without excess paint building up. When the first wall is complete, allow it to dry thoroughly before taping it off to paint the adjoining wall.

paint the room

Paint the room from the top down: the ceiling first, then the walls, trim, baseboards, and doors, and finally the floor.

the base coat

Once you have prepared and, if necessary, primed the surfaces, you are ready to paint the base coat. For solid coverage, apply two coats and let the first dry before applying the second. If the base coat is a dark color, you may require a third coat. (Remember you can tint the primer to help get solid coverage for dark colors.)

The base coat is applied either as the finishing color for the room or as the base color for a paint effect to be applied over it. This is the point at which the project instructions begin.

The base coat sheen is generally flat for the ceiling, satin for the walls, and semigloss for the baseboards and trim. Higher sheens are easier to clean, but they also show up imperfections.

To help paint a clean edge, use a cutting-in brush, which has angled bristles. If the ceiling is stucco, or if the edges between the walls and the ceiling are uneven, apply tape 1/2" down from the ceiling to get a straight stopping point.

Use a ladder to cut in around the ceiling perimeter. Attach an extension pole to a paint roller to fill in the ceiling. Use ceiling paint if you are not going to apply a paint finish to the ceiling. Otherwise use regular latex paint.

When the ceiling is dry, retape to get a nice clean edge for the walls. Cut in along the ceiling line and around the trim first. Then roll the paint on the wall in a W, going back and forth to remove roller marks. Don't overload your brush or roller. You will get better results by applying two thin, even coats because there is less chance of dripping.

When the walls are dry, tape them off and paint the trim and baseboards. Paint in the direction of the wood grain, or the length of the trim if there is no grain.

If you are painting the floor, remove the quarter-round molding if possible and paint it separately. Tape off around the baseboards. Cut in around the perimeter as you did with the walls, and then fill in with a roller. Remember to start at the farthest point from the door and work toward the door. Apply the paint in the direction of the wood planks.

If you are staining the floor, wear gloves. Soak a smooth rag in the stain and rub the stain over the wood in the direction of the grain. Wipe off the excess to keep an even depth. Once the first coat dries, another coat can be applied until you achieve the color you want.

applying a paint effect

Now the fun begins. In the bedrooms that follow, I have demonstrated some of my favorite paint effects. They all have their own personality and offer a range of looks from soft and sultry veiling (page 127 to glitzy gilding (page 76) and manly flannel (page 82). Follow the step-by-step instructions and you will be delighted at how easily these effects take form. But there is one golden rule when applying a paint effect to a

large surface such as a wall. You must keep a wet edge or you will end up with a patchwork pattern of dried edges that will ruin your design.

When you are applying a paint effect that requires blending different colors or creating patterns in the paint with rags or other tools, the paint must stay wet long enough to be manipulated. Latex paint dries very quickly, so this is where the water-based glazing liquid comes in. It does not change the color of your paint, but makes it translucent and slows down the drying time to give you more time to work.

When applying a paint effect it is necessary to work in manageable patches, about 3 or 4 square feet at a time. As you move along, the edges of the patches must remain wet so that as you overlap the paint or glaze for the next section, it can be manipulated in the same way. If the edges have dried, you will get lap marks or lines around the patches.

Work on one wall at a time and tape off the adjoining walls so that you won't get paint buildup in the corners. Begin at the top of the wall and work down to the bottom, then return to the top and so on until you have finished the wall. Apply the colored glaze to the first patch, work the effect, and then apply the colored glaze to the next section, overlapping the edge slightly to ensure that it is wet. Work the effect starting at the edge and complete that patch. Continue in this manner until the wall is complete. If you find that an edge has dried by the time you return to it, applying some clear glaze should open it up again, but it is important to work quickly. The best method is to work with a partner, one person applying the glaze and the other working the effect.

paint the furniture

Once the piece is prepared and primed, apply two coats of the base-coat color. This may be the finish for the piece, or the background for a paint effect. Either way it is important that the paint is applied smoothly, without drips and visible brush marks. This is best accomplished by applying thin coats of paint and not overloading your paintbrush.

For a dresser, if you haven't already done so, remove the drawers and the hardware. If there are legs on the dresser, turn the piece upside down and paint them first. Once dry, turn the piece right side up and paint the body, then the top. Paint the faces of the drawers separately. Keep paint away from any of the running surfaces—the top edges of the drawers and the inside edges of the spaces where the drawers are inserted into the dresser.

Varnish is not necessary unless you are protecting a paint effect or a dresser top from extra wear and tear.

Bedside tables are painted the same way as dressers.

Turn wooden chairs upside down and paint the legs first, applying the paint from the lower leg toward the seat and any rungs. Watch for drips, especially around any tool work or spindles. Turn the chair upright and paint the back rungs or slats first, then the seat.

Varnish is not necessary.

bedroom makeovers

Each of these bedrooms was designed for and with the real homeowner. When creating a new bedroom, my inspiration comes from an element that the inhabitant loves. Whether it is a favorite color, a piece of furniture, or a specific style, I want to discover what will make her or his heart sing. That could mean using a collection of angels for Guardian Angel on page 102, or designing a bed that is sleek, contemporary, and provides the owner with an oasis for a day of leisure, such as the platform bed on page 98. A very small bedroom needed a masculine touch to suit a young man on a slim budget in Gentlemen Prefer Flannel, page 82. And the color and drama of Italy, a frequent vacation destination, heated up a large but bland bedroom for a couple in Grand Opera, page 120.

All these rooms incorporate at least one how-to project, whether it is a paint finish for the walls, staining or painting a floor, or making your own furniture. You may wish to replicate a room style from top to bottom or take one idea from one makeover and adapt it for your own bedroom. If you follow the instructions, everything can be achieved by even the first-time do-it-yourselfer. Your reward for the time spent planning, shopping, and painting will be a personal and comforting environment created especially for you.

plantation
bedroom

A therapeutic trip to Jamaica was the inspiration behind this bedroom. My good friend Robin had just been through an unpleasant divorce. As she began to rebuild her life, I decided that redecorating her bedroom would help her make a great new start. The room itself is bright, with a high ceiling and a broad turret in one corner, which makes an interesting architectural detail.

We visited Jamaica and explored the island's many plantation houses, which were built by the sugar barons of the eighteenth and nineteenth centuries. These homes were initially simple in design, but as the sugar barons' wealth grew, their homes became increasingly stately. Great stone pillars marked the entranceways. The interiors were typically dark, as the hot Caribbean sun was kept out by shutters—this is where the term *plantation shutters* was coined. These vast homes were often built high in the hills, to catch the cool breezes. Many had open latticework around the top of the exterior walls to allow any fresh breeze to ventilate the rooms.

I repeated the designs of pillars and latticework in the bedroom, using stencils. The walls were painted in the coolest Caribbean Sea green to offset the richly stained mahogany floor. A magnificent four-poster bed dominates the room, and an antique lace bedspread adds to the romance. The unusual curved windows need to be only partially covered for privacy. Painted wood shutters allow the light to dance through by day. This bedroom may be many long miles away from island life, but it still achieves the same tranquil spirit.

lattice border

The walls are 11 feet high, but there are no ceiling moldings to bring the room down to scale. I solved this by using an oversized lattice stencil to make the proportions of the room more pleasing. The walls were first painted in Caribbean Sea green, leaving an 18-inch band of white below the ceiling for the lattice. The stencil has two parts, including a method of applying a shadow that creates a three-dimensional illusion. The pillars were stenciled in each corner in several tones of white and gray. These giant stencils have many layers and it does take time to accomplish the effect of a real pillar, but the actual process is easy.

MATERIALS AND TOOLS

light seafoam green and white latex
   paint, satin

roller and paint tray

measuring tape

chalk line

pencil

low-tack painter's tape

two-part lattice stencil (see Resources)

spray adhesive

periwinkle blue and dark seafoam
   green stencil paint

2 stencil brushes

For best results, prepare your surface following the instructions in the preparation section, page 44.

step 1   Apply 2 base coats of light seafoam green and let dry overnight.

step 2   Use the chalk line to mark off an 18″ border around the top of the wall (where the lattice will be) and tape it off. Apply 2 coats of white paint to the border section. Let it dry overnight.

step 3   Take the first stencil overlay, spray the back with stencil adhesive, and place it into position on the wall. Use low-tack painter's tape to secure it firmly. Fill in the registration marks with pencil. This is very important. You will need these marks as you move the stencil along, and also to line up your second overlay.

step 4 *(Shot 1)* With a stencil brush and periwinkle blue stencil paint, lightly shade in either side of the lattice squares. Do not fill in the whole square, but feather the paint toward the center, leaving the middle white. Lift the stencil and move it along, using the registration marks to realign it. Continue in this manner all around the border.

step 5 *(Shot 2)* Spray the back of the second lattice stencil overlay and place it into position, again using the registration marks as your guide. With dark seafoam green paint, stencil in the alternate squares. Apply the green a little heavier on the outside of each square, and lighter in the middle. Let dry completely.

four-poster bed

I wanted a four-poster bed that would suit the elegance of this plantation-style bedroom, but they were prohibitively expensive. My carpenter, Mr. K., came up with a design that could be built using wood right off the shelf from the lumber store. We used simply carved newel posts, meant for a stair railing, for our bed posts, and attached them to lengths of 4″ × 4″s with epoxy glue to add the required height. Once the bed frame was assembled I stained it the same gorgeous deep mahogany as the floor. For added panache I screwed large gold pineapple finials, originally designed for the ends of curtain rods, to the top of each newel post.

colonial floor

MATERIALS AND TOOLS

*mahogany and ebony or dark brown
    wood stain*

mixing container

soft, clean, lint-free rags

latex gloves

metal ruler

pencil

low-tack painter's tape

X-acto knife

drop cloth (optional)

high-gloss acrylic varnish

varnish brush or foam roller

For best results, prepare your surface following the instructions in the preparation section, page 44.

Note: If you are staining a new, raw wood floor, sand the surface first to open the wood's pores so that it will take the stain evenly.

step 1   (*Shot 1*) Pour some mahogany stain into a mixing container. Wearing gloves, dip a folded rag into the stain and apply it to the floor boards. Start in the corner farthest from the doorway. Work in sections, applying the stain to cover the surface completely, and then going back to wipe off the excess. Wipe in the direction of the grain. Leave the floor to dry overnight.

step 2   (*Shot 2*) Our dark borders are 9″ wide and 1¼″ wide. Measure in from the wall, draw a pencil line as a guide, and then mark off the border sections with tape. Press the tape down hard all along the edges and in the grooves between the planks. To keep the dark stain from bleeding under the tape, place a metal ruler or straightedge along the edge of the tape and score the line with the X-acto knife.

step 3   (*Shot 3*) Lay down a drop cloth to protect the rest of the floor from spatters, as stain is impossible to remove. Using a fresh clean folded rag, apply the dark brown stain to the border stripes as in step 1. Let dry.

step 4   (*Shot 4*) Remove the tape. Apply 3 coats of clear acrylic varnish for protection. Leave the floor to cure for 4 to 5 days, depending on heat and humidity, before moving furniture back.

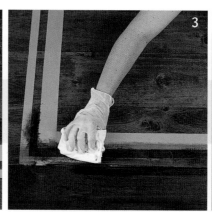

Mahogany once grew in abundance on the island of Jamaica, and therefore most of the furnishings and floors were made from this gorgeous hardwood. Today, mahogany has become scarce, and very expensive, but we can still get the look of this rare, rich-looking wood with mahogany-colored stain. Although the floors in the plantation homes were traditionally made from wide planks, I managed to reproduce the grandeur on this bedroom's existing hardwood floor by staining it in a deep reddish brown with an ebony striped border. Three coats of high-gloss varnish make an elegant finish.

her sanctuary

Christina has a hectic life with three little girls under the age of five. I remember those days well. Up at the crack of dawn, rarely a minute to yourself, and falling into bed after the last child succumbs to sleep. Christina desperately wanted a space of her own where she could curl up with a book or magazine, even if only for a few stolen minutes. This bedroom has plenty of natural light, but was bland and far from comforting. I chose a palette of calming café au lait, whipped cream, and chocolate. The room is framed with pure white curtains and painted molding. The walls were embellished with an oversized swirling leaf border taken from the pattern on the duvet cover. Instead of using paint, we penciled the design onto the wall with a collection of colored pencils. The effect is muted and delicate, embracing the dreamy quality we wanted for her sanctuary.

The bedroom has a nonworking fireplace, but I left it in, in case Christina wanted to open it up at a later date, and decorated the opening with cutoff logs creating the illusion of stacked wood. The finishing touch was a joint project. Christina's eldest daughter, Erica, and I took an artist's canvas and layered it with a couple of coats of gesso. Once it was dry, we stenciled the word *dream* in relief using a thicker layer of gesso. Christina loves her new room—and so do the children!

before

dream canvas

*artist's canvas on stretcher frame and
 primed (you can order any dimensions
 you need from an art supply store)*

ornamental gesso (see Resources)

spatula

light beige latex paint, satin

water-based glazing liquid

mixing container

2" paintbrush

soft, clean, lint-free rags

*photocopies or prints of the letters D, R,
 E, A, and M*

Mylar

indelible marker

cutting mat

X-acto knife

fine-grade sandpaper (optional)

RECIPE

1 part latex paint

3 parts water-based glazing liquid

Throughout the entire makeover, Christina's five-year-old was itching to help. Once the walls were complete, Erica joined me in making a large piece of art for over the bed. We bought an artist's canvas, prestretched and primed, from an art supply store. Gesso is a type of plaster that has an elastic quality. It's used by artists as the base for their work, creating a smooth surface to paint on. Gesso is usually applied in a thin, smooth coat, but we troweled on the gesso in waves and ridges, creating a textured background. (If plaster of Paris or stucco is used, the plaster will crack into fine lines when applied in a thick coat. With gesso, you can get a textured surface that is still silky smooth.) Once the first layer was dry, I applied a very thin wash of beige paint over the surface to lightly highlight the texture of the plaster. Then, using more gesso, we stenciled the word *dream* in the center of the canvas. We applied the gesso with our fingers, thickly over each letter, and when the stencil was removed, the white letters stood up in relief.

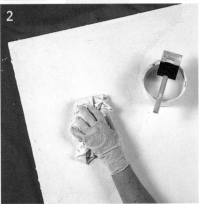

Our dimensions are 24″ × 30″.

step 1 (*Shot 1*) Apply a fairly thin layer of gesso with a spatula, covering the canvas completely. Build up a nice texture by crossing your strokes and varying the pressure on the spatula.

step 2 (*Shot 2*) Mix the colored glaze according to the recipe. Apply the glaze to the canvas evenly. Rub and blend out the brush marks with a soft rag and let dry.

step 3 (*Shot 3*) To make the letter stencils, print out the word *dream* from your computer or use a photocopier to get the size letters you want. Trace the letters onto Mylar with the marker and cut them out. With the letters D, R, and A, normally you would cut bridges in the stencil to hold in the interior pieces, but because we are using gesso to fill in the stencil, bridges would be too difficult to fill in later. So cut out these letters completely, and then tape the center parts down on the canvas in position inside their corresponding letters.

step 4 (*Shot 4*) Center the stencil letters on the canvas and tape them down. Dip your fingers into the gesso, and fill in the letters, being careful not to get any underneath the stencil.

step 5 (*Shot 5*) Remove the stencil when it is properly filled in and let dry overnight.

step 6 If you feel that the texture on the dried letters is too jagged, give them a light sanding.

sheer delight

The existing venetian blinds block out the light and allow for privacy, but they are hard and clinical in such a sensuous room. I left them in place, but added a layer of white transparent sheers. I hung the fabric from loops of satin ribbon over a row of ornamental drawer pulls.

fake fireplace logs

This is not a working fireplace. The hole insert is only a few inches deep and is painted black. To add visual interest, I built a stack of logs, sized to fit the narrow opening. Real logs were cut into 3″ slices. To make it safer for this young family, I glued the wood pile together so that it would not tumble down.

pencil stencil

The design was traced onto a roll of craft paper. Small holes were made along the lines of the pattern and then the paper was taped to the wall. Using a pencil, I marked through the holes and then removed the paper. The dots were joined up, creating the pattern on the wall. Colored pencils are completely nontoxic and simple to use. There is no cleanup and you can work at your own pace, coming back to fill in more of the pattern when you have free time. Any mistakes are simply erased. I selected a monochromatic palette of earthy browns; the rolling swirls make a soothing landscape for tired eyes.

MATERIALS AND TOOLS

design

graph paper

pencil

ruler

roll of craft paper

X-acto knife

low-tack painter's tape

non-water-soluble colored pencils (we used brown, black, bronze, dark red, and gray)

pencil sharpener

eraser

matte spray varnish

face mask

step 1   (*Shot 1*) To make the template for your design, first trace or draw it freehand onto a piece of graph paper.

step 2   (*Shot 2*) To increase the picture to the right proportion for your wall, draw a large grid on the craft paper and transfer the design to scale.

step 3   Use the X-acto knife to cut tiny slits along the lines of the design.

step 4   (*Shot 3*) Tape the craft paper into position on the wall. Draw light pencil marks through the slits you made with the knife around the design.

step 5   Remove the paper and connect the pencil marks to complete the picture on the wall.

step 6   (*Shot 4*) Color in the design with the colored pencils. Hold the pencil as you would normally for writing. Using the pencil tip, scribble back and forth lightly so that you don't get obvious lines. Pencil in the areas you want shaded with more scribbles, but don't press down any harder. Sharpen the tip periodically and remove any mistakes with an eraser.

step 7   Apply a coat of spray varnish in the same sheen as basecoat to protect your work. Brushing varnish over the colored pencil, even though it is non-water-soluble, may cause it to blur. Always wear a mask when using spray varnish and work in a well-ventilated area.

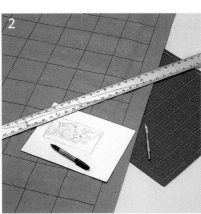
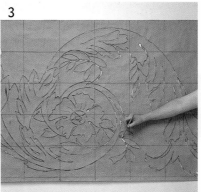

putting on the glitz

I had a blank canvas to work with in Sam's bedroom. His desire was a room that was comfortable, contemporary, and glamorous. These three challenges were all addressed by making an oversized headboard from lengths of ornate stock molding. For pure luxury, I gilded the carved surface of the molding with a lilac-colored metallic leaf. This frames a padded piece of brushed velvet that is both soft and sexy. The budget was tight, so I took two plain bedside tables and silver-leafed the tops. These two ugly ducklings became beautiful swans with new hardware and a glamorous finish. When I first approached Sam with the idea of a lilac bedroom, he was tongue-tied. But there are many variations of this color, from purple to lavender, and here I used the palest dove gray. It's fresh and soothing, and Sam was delighted with his new room.

before

gilded headboard

MATERIALS AND TOOLS

canvas on a stretcher frame (art supply stores will make a stretcher to your dimensions)

fiberfill padding, enough to cover the canvas

scissors

spray adhesive

stretch velvet

staple gun

frame molding (the back of the molding strips have an L-shape cut out of the inside edges to permit the picture to be set in)

aquasize

small brush

colored metallic leaf (see Resources)

soft brush

nails or screws

hammer or screwdriver

picture hanging kit

Gilding is an elaborate art form that has been used for centuries to dress up moldings and furnishings. The traditional technique involves years of practice to become an expert, but today there are easier methods for simple home use. One of my favorite simplifications is the option of replacing gold size, a sticky varnish designed to attach the metallic leaf to the surface, with an adhesive transfer paper. This method was used on the bedside tabletop seen on page 80, but is not suitable to use on a frame with lots of detail. Instead, aquasize is applied to the painted surface. Traditionally, metallic leaf was available in gold, silver, copper, and bronze. Now art supply stores have many wonderful metallic colors. I chose a luscious lilac for the frame of this oversized headboard. Stock molding in a floral design was cut to size, given a base coat of paint, and then leafed. Inside the frame, inexpensive nylon velvet was pulled over a canvas stretcher that was covered in padding. The effect is both luxurious and comfortable.

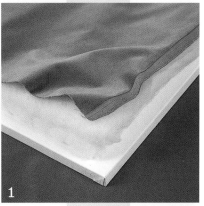

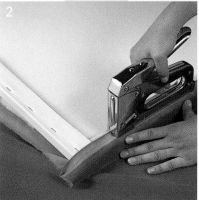

step 1   (*Shot 1*) Spray the canvas on the stretcher frame with adhesive and adhere 1 or 2 layers of fiberfill. Cut the velvet to fit plus enough to turn around the edges to the back.

step 2   (*Shot 2*) Stretch the velvet over the top and staple it to the back of the frame.

step 3   Assemble your decorative molding frame to fit over the velvet headboard.

step 4   (*Shot 3*) To gild the frame, apply aquasize with a brush, making sure to get into all the indentations.

step 5   (*Shot 4*) Once the aquasize is tacky to the touch, gently place a piece of the leaf on top. Brush it smooth with a soft brush, and let dry for 15 to 60 minutes, depending on the product and humidity.

step 6   (*Shot 5*) Use the soft dry brush to brush gently over the leaf, getting rid of any loose bits.

step 7   Attach the frame to the velvet headboard with nails or screws.

step 8   Hang the headboard on the wall as you would a framed piece of art.

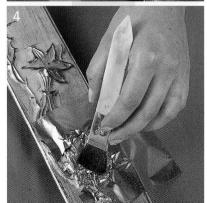

foiled bedside tables

I bought Sam a pair of inexpensive bed-side tables from an unfinished-wood furniture store. Rather than having to sand down old paint and varnish drips, the only preparation required was a coat of wood primer to seal the wood. The tables were given a simple charcoal base coat, but it's the tops that make the pieces special. A new technique uses dry adhesive transfers to adhere a metallic pattern to the surface. Here we used a Greek key design.

MATERIALS AND TOOLS

raw wood bedside table
sandpaper (optional)
tack cloth (optional)
wood primer
small roller and paint tray
charcoal latex paint, satin
aquasize
foam brush
silver leaf
soft brush
dry size transfer, border pattern (see Resources)
burnishing tool or wooden end of a paintbrush
lavender metallic leaf (see Resources)
acrylic spray varnish
semigloss acrylic varnish
varnish brush or foam brush

For best results, prepare your surface following the instructions in the preparation section, page 44.

step 1 Lightly sand the table if necessary, and wipe off any dust with a tack cloth. Apply a coat of primer; let dry.

step 2 (Shot 1) Apply 2 base coats of charcoal and let dry overnight.

step 3 (Shot 2) Apply aquasize over the top and edges of the table. Wait until it dries to the tacky stage, about 10 to 15 minutes.

step 4 (Shot 3) Gently lay the silver leaf over the tabletop and edges, and smooth it down with a soft dry brush. Let dry for 1 to 4 hours, depending on the humidity and the product you are using.

step 5   (*Shot 4*) Once it's dry, go over the leaf again with the soft brush to remove any excess, leaving a smooth silver surface.

step 6   (*Shot 5*) Line up the dry size border pattern so that it runs straight around the perimeter of the table, about 1″ from the edge. Lay the pattern adhesive side down. Rub with a burnishing tool to transfer the adhesive to the tabletop. Remove the pattern.

step 7   (*Shot 6*) Lay lavender metallic leaf over the dry size and smooth it down gently with the soft brush. Brush away any excess.

step 8   Seal the top with varnish. Use spray varnish for the first coat to protect the leaf. Then finish with the liquid. Let dry completely.

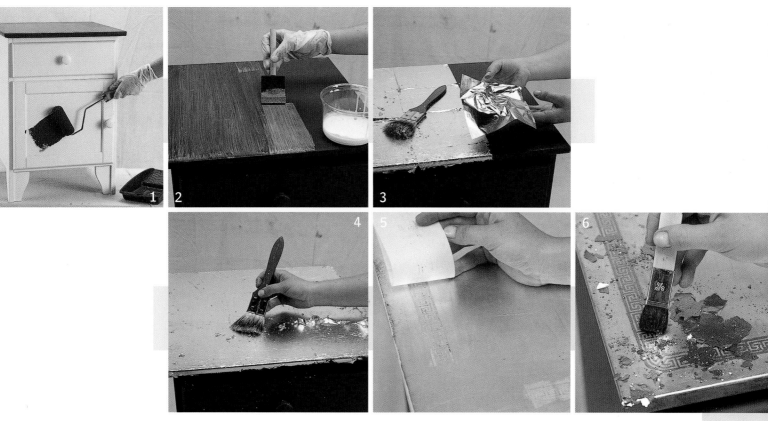

gentlemen prefer flannel

One of the most interesting areas of London to visit is the cluster of small streets around St. James. Here you will find gentlemen's shops that have the gentility and refinement of a previous age. They are filled with quality cloths for tailoring men's suits: a vast selection of pinstripes, houndstooth checks, and flannels in every possible tone of gray, navy, black, and brown. There is great beauty in both the luxurious texture and the subtle hues of these fine fabrics. The home decorating industry has now discovered their richness and these fabrics are being used to upholster furniture and for curtains, cushions and even bedding.

When I was asked to decorate this young man's bedroom, I turned to these tailored fabrics for inspiration. The walls were textured with a rough tinted plaster in a manly gray. The room was plain, with no moldings or trim, so I edged each wall and corner with a paint effect to give the illusion that lengths of grosgrain ribbon finished off each wall. The curtains were made from charcoal flannel and finished with beautifully designed school-blazer buttons. Martin had inherited a series of framed prints, so I hung them in a geometric pattern and linked the frames together with ribbon. Carrying on the theme of men's fabrics, I took his dated '70s wood-veneer desk and painted it to replicate pinstripe cloth. The bed was piled with pillows and cushions made from these tailored fabrics and accessorized with suede buttons. The mix of texture and pattern is a pleasing blend of masculinity and softness.

before

suitable walls

MATERIALS AND TOOLS

Durabond-90

gray and black latex paint, satin

mixing container

4" paintbrush

foam stucco roller

ruler

chalk

low-tack painter's tape

1" paintbrush

metal or rubber combing tool

Today's trend for textured walls has come a long way from unsophisticated stucco. We can now reproduce the delicate softness of suede and the suppleness of leather with the numerous plaster products on the market. For these walls, I created the nap felt in men's flannel by mixing Durabond-90 with the paint and then rolled with a stucco roller. The fine texture adds interest to an otherwise completely plain wall. Because there are no decorative features to this boxy room, I painted the illusion of grosgrain ribbon along the top of each wall, and where the walls meet at the corners. For clean, neat corners, do each side separately and let each side dry thoroughly before taping over it. To replicate the look of grosgrain ribbon I painted the strips black, and immediately combed through the wet paint, creating the straight weave found in the ribbon.

For best results, prepare your surface following the guidelines in the preparation section, page 44.

step 1   Mix equal parts of Durabond and gray paint. Stir well.

step 2   (*Shot 1*) Working in 3′ sections, apply the mixture to the wall with a large paintbrush.

step 3   (*Shot 2*) While it is still wet, roll over the section with the stucco roller, flattening out any brush marks and creating the texture of flannel.

step 4   Continue working in sections until the walls are covered.

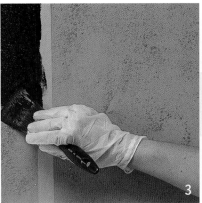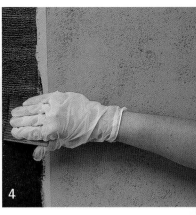

1 2 3 4

step 5   (*Shot 3*) Measure and mark off a 1½" border down each corner edge and around the ceiling. Chalk will show up against the gray paint. Use painter's tape to tape off the border, pressing down hard along the edge of the tape. Working in 5′ lengths, use the small brush to apply black paint along the border.

step 6   (*Shot 4*) Immediately go over the paint with a comb, pulling down vertically along the ceiling borders and pulling across horizontally along the wall border. This will give the impression of grosgrain ribbon. Let dry and remove the tape.

blazer button tabs

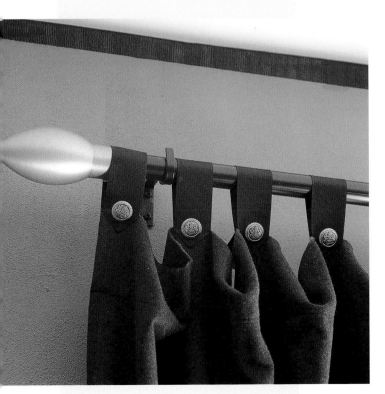

These are simply sewn curtains made from 2 lengths of gray flannel. The edges were hemmed and then a length of grosgrain ribbon was stitched down the outside edge of each panel to match the paint trim on the walls. The ribbon was also used to hang the curtains, sewn as loops across the tops of the panels and secured with blazer buttons.

pinstripe desktop

This flat veneer desk was ideal for a pinstripe makeover. The piece you are painting in this effect should be as smooth and plain as possible, with no ornamentation. All you need is two coats of a dark color, one used in men's pinstriped suits, such as navy, gray, or black. Once dry, apply the fine white pinstripes with a ruler and sharp chalk pencil. To seal in the chalk, the surface must be sprayed with clear varnish.

1

MATERIALS AND TOOLS

medium- and fine-grade sandpaper

tack cloth

high-adhesion primer

black latex paint, satin

mixing container

2 small rollers and paint trays

long metal ruler

dressmaker's chalk pencil

matte acrylic spray varnish

face mask

For best results, prepare your surface following the instructions in the preparation section, page 44.

step 1 Sand the desktop and wipe it clean with a tack cloth. Pour some primer into the mixing container and add a bit of black paint to tint it to gray. Apply the primer and let dry.

step 2 Apply 2 coats of black paint. For solid coverage with dark colors you may need to add a third coat. Let dry for 4 hours.

step 3 (Shot 1) Mark off 2" stripes along the width of the desktop. With dressmaker's chalk and a long ruler, draw out the pinstripes.

step 4 You must use spray varnish to protect your work, as brushing over the chalk lines will blur or erase them. Always wear a mask when spraying, and work in a well-ventilated area.

continental cushions

For this young man's room we used the same flannel as the curtains for one of the pillows. Cut the front piece 2″ wider than the back and make a 1″ pleat with the excess fabric down the middle. Sew the pleat closed, press it flat to the fabric, and sew buttons down the pleat to resemble a button fly on an old-fashioned pair of trousers.

The pocket pillow is sewn with 3 equal-sized pieces of pinstripe fabric. The pocket piece is turned over about 3″ from the top and trimmed with 2 lines of white stitching.

As a final touch, standard white pillowcases were trimmed with the same grosgrain ribbon used on the curtains.

houndstooth dresser

A flat-fronted chest of drawers was first painted white, and then a houndstooth pattern was stenciled over the top. To make the stencil I photocopied and enlarged the design from a piece of fabric, then cut a stencil from Mylar.

radiant blue

Most people choose blue when asked their favorite color. It's familiar and comforting, probably because it is always around us in the many hues of the sky and the ocean. All blues, from lavender to aqua, radiate a natural energy. Teamed with white, blue brings a classic combination of clarity and freshness to a room. It's exactly what was needed when I was asked to do this bedroom makeover. The owners wanted to keep their furniture. Although tired and dated, the dresser, headboard, and bedside tables were well made; they just needed a new look. A couple of coats of pure white trimmed with cobalt blue and they were immediately transformed. The walls were painted in the deepest indigo and lighter tones of blue were washed over the surface. The technique was taken a step further by using the dark base and painting a mural with lighter shades of blue. Although a mural is daunting for many people, a similar feeling is created by just color-washing all the walls from dark to light. I'm not usually a huge fan of parquet flooring, but the patterned squares make the ideal base for mapping out a painted rug.

before

midnight sky walls

MATERIALS AND TOOLS

indigo blue, dark blue, and pale blue
latex paint, satin

low-tack painter's tape

water-based glazing liquid

2 foam rollers and paint trays

mixing containers

soft, clean, lint-free rags

stippling brush or stiff bristle brush

RECIPE

1 part latex paint
2 parts water-based glazing liquid

For best results prepare your surface following the instructions in the preparation section, page 44.

step 1   Apply 2 base coats of indigo blue and let dry for 4 hours.

step 2   Work on one wall at a time. Tape off the wall along the connecting corners. Mix a dark and a light blue colored glaze according to the recipe.

step 3   (*Shot 1*) Work in 4' square patches and keep a wet edge (see page 58). With the foam roller, apply the darker blue glaze loosely over the surface, allowing some of the base coat to show through.

step 4   (*Shot 2*) Immediately dab the surface with a rag to get rid of any obvious roller marks.

step 5   (*Shot 3*) While the glaze is still wet, go over the surface in random patches with the pale blue glaze. Dab with a clean rag to soften any hard lines.

step 6   (*Shot 4*) Stipple the surface to blend and add texture.

step 7   Move to the next section and repeat the technique. If the edges are dry, apply clear glaze to open the paint.

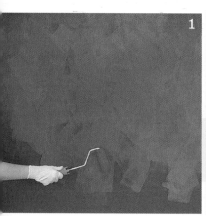
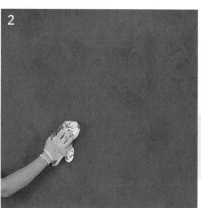

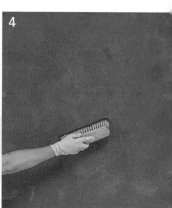

rollered mural

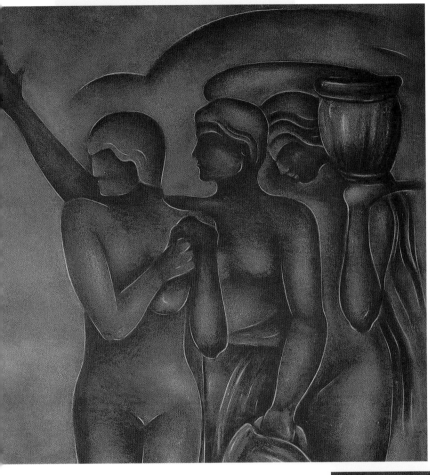

Once the walls were painted in a color-wash of deep blues, a mural was sketched out with chalk. You can blow up a design from a book on a photocopier to trace onto the wall, or use a projector, or if you are not comfortable with these solutions, call your local art college and ask a student to help you out. The artist who painted this stunning mural used rollers to make the images with a dark blue for the outlines of the figures graduating to a light blue for highlighting.

Traditionally most paint finishes start with a light base and then a slightly darker color is color-washed, ragged, or dragged over the surface. Occasionally it is preferable to start with a dark base and go lighter. When a very dark color, as in this case a deep indigo blue, is applied as a base, and mid-tone blues are rubbed over the top, the effect is like a midnight sky.

paint underfoot

To avoid having to strip the whole parquet floor, I just mapped out the shape of the eventual rug and taped off the area. This was then sanded and primed. Once the white base coat was dry, I created the pattern using the shapes in the parquet. The taping did take a long time, but the painting was very fast, and once the tape was removed the effect was stunning. The finishing touch for a real trompe l'oeil rug is to hand-paint a fringe at either end.

MATERIALS AND TOOLS

low-tack painter's tape

X-acto knife

medium-grade sandpaper

high-adhesion primer

roller and paint tray

2 small rollers and paint trays

white, beige, and sky blue latex paint,
    satin

mixing container

¼″ and fine artist's brushes

satin or gloss acrylic varnish

varnish brush or foam brush

step 1   Tape off the area you want to paint. Sand the surface to rough up the shiny finish. Wipe clean. Apply 2 coats of primer, and 2 base coats of white.

step 2   (Shot 1) Tape off the design you want. You will be able to see the grooves between the parquet tiles through the white base coat, so you can use these as a guide. It's not necessary to measure, so the taping is easier than it looks. Use a sharp knife to cut the tape for nice clean edges. Make sure the tape is pressed down firmly.

step 3   (Shot 2) Fill in the carpet with beige paint. To prevent leakage, apply the paint in thin coats.

step 4   (Shot 3) Remove the tape as soon as possible after painting. If any paint has leaked under the tape, wipe it off with a damp cloth.

step 5   (Shot 4) Mix a little beige and white paint. Use a ¼″ artist's brush to apply a background shadow for the fringe. Let dry.

step 6   (Shot 5) With the ¼″ brush, paint a tassel fringe over the shadow. Then dip a fine artist's brush into the blue paint and draw in blue threads.

step 7   Once the painted carpet is dry, apply 4 coats of varnish for protection. Allow a week for the carpet to cure before walking on it.

tufted headboard

MATERIALS AND TOOLS

white latex paint, flat
2″ paintbrush
right-angle ruler
pencil
penny
cobalt blue artist's acrylic
plastic plate
artist's brush
cup of water
matte or satin acrylic varnish
varnish brush or foam brush

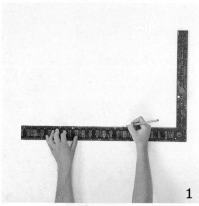

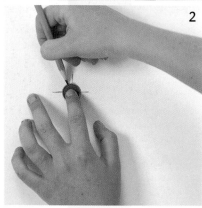

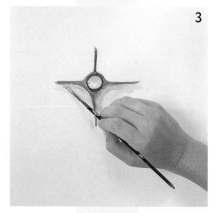

For best results, prepare your surface following the instructions in the preparation section, page 44.

step 1   Apply 2 base coats of white and let dry for 4 hours.

step 2   (*Shot 1*) Mark out where the buttons will go on each panel of the headboard. We had 3 panels, and put 4 buttons evenly spaced on each panel. Use a right-angle ruler to line them up evenly.

step 3   (*Shot 2*) Draw a "+" to mark where the buttons will go and extend the lines so that they are longer than the width of a penny. Center the penny over the + and trace around it. Use the ruler to extend the lines 2½″ from the center of the penny.

step 4   Put a blob of cobalt blue artist's acrylic and a small amount of white latex paint on the plate. The button and tufting around the button are shaded according to the light source in the room. If the window is on the left side of the bed, then the right side of the button will be lighter, and so forth.

step 5   Paint the button first. Dip the artist's brush into the water and then mix with a bit of the blue paint. Paint the outline of the button. Now create shading inside and around the outline of the button by mixing the blue with white to get a lighter and lighter shade.

step 6   (*Shot 3*) Paint in the tuft lines darker near the button, then fading out. Add white to the blue for shading as in step 5. Shade in the arc shape darker close to the button and fading out.

step 7   Repeat the painted arc at the corners of the headboard to give the appearance of padded rounded corners.

step 8   When all the tufting is painted, let dry for 4 hours and then apply 2 coats of varnish for protection.

Furniture built in the '40s and '50s is usually solid and well made, but with these pieces the finish is definitely of another era. A fresh coat of paint will do marvels to give them new life. By painting all the mismatched furnishings white, they are immediately unified, and you become more aware of their beautiful shapes. White brings a heightened awareness of color, texture, and shape. This headboard was painted to create the illusion of tufted fabric. It's easy to do, but the effect is so real that admirers automatically have to run their hands over the surface to check the authenticity. Any shape headboard will suffice.

sheer
magic

Anita wished to bring her love of clean, modern design to the rugged interior of her urban loft. Light spills into the bedroom through oversized windows that open onto a busy city square. The challenge was to design a rhythm between the heavy brick walls and the bright open space. Our first task was her bed. To relax and recharge after a long work week, Anita likes to spend a good part of her day off in bed, sipping coffee, reading, and snoozing. We asked our carpenter to design a platform bed that would be an island unto itself. Using drywall, pine, and MDF, he constructed a self-contained unit, a contemporary bed with smooth sleek lines that incorporates shelving and bedside tables—perfect for Anita's needs. To bring the high ceilings down to cozier proportions, I hung the lighting low on either side of the bed.

The natural light comes from huge windows, which I covered with panels of patterned sheers hung from swing arms because the windows open like doors. The walls around the windows are drywall, not brick. I created an interesting paint technique to highlight this area with the same delicate texture as the sheers. This bedroom demonstrates how a combination of different surfaces can work together successfully.

before

platform bed

To bring the height of the loft walls down to a more pleasing scale, we made the bed's back wall one-third as high as the walls. Glass shelves are built into either side for books, candles, and picture frames. The bed frame is constructed from 8″ × 2″ pine and the edges and platform are MDF. This gives a silky smooth surface ready for a shiny finish. I chose celadon green paint, a modern shade that is both calming and vibrant. The glass-like sheen was produced by applying a coat of epoxy varnish over the paint. One coat of epoxy varnish is the equivalent of many coats of regular varnish. It is now available in less toxic water-based form. See Resources (page 172).

pop art

Andy Warhol was a pioneer of the art form that repeats the same image over and over again. We adapted this technique by taking a beautiful head shot of Anita and blowing it up on a photocopier until we had just one section of her face— her gorgeous eyes. This image was then copied in color. We managed to match the same celadon green we used on the bed platform. Instead of framing the pictures, they were sized to fit standard 6″ × 8″ plastic folders, and were put up on the wall with suction cups that were attached to bullnose clips.

whimsical window frame

MATERIALS AND TOOLS

caramel and white latex paint, satin

roller and paint tray

measuring tape

roll of fax paper

spray adhesive

water-based glazing liquid

mixing container

foam roller and paint tray

RECIPE

1 part latex paint

1 part water-based glazing liquid

For best results prepare your surface following the instructions in the preparation section, page 44.

step 1　Apply 2 base coats of caramel to the bedroom walls, stopping about 1′ from the window edges. Let dry completely.

step 2　(*Shot 1*) Rip a piece of fax paper off the roll to a length approximately the same as the height of the window. Rip this piece down the middle; you want a ragged edge. Rip a piece of paper to go along the top of the window as well. Apply spray adhesive to the back of the paper and stick it all around the frame of the window with the flat side against the window edge. Rip the corners so they are loosely mitered and form a jagged frame corner.

step 3　(*Shot 2*) Continue to paint the walls with caramel, rolling it over the paper. Apply 2 coats as you have on the rest of the walls. Let dry for 4 hours and remove the paper.

step 4　(*Shot 3*) Make sure any paint on the paper is dry. Turn it over, spray the painted side, and reapply the paper strips to the wall so that the jagged edge is facing the window frame and is showing approximately 2″ of the caramel color. Mix the white glaze according to the recipe. Roll the glaze over the exposed area between the paper and the window's edge. The glaze allows the caramel to show through, creating a sheer effect. Remove the paper and let dry.

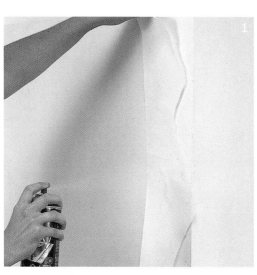
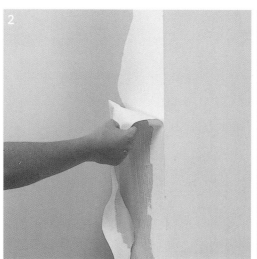

The windows in this loft bedroom are very high, rising floor to ceiling. I replaced the existing blinds with sheer fabric hung from swing arm rods, which makes a very clean and contemporary look. There was no frame around the window, so I painted a delicate design using fax paper as a template. The strip around the window is painted pure white, and the second strip is white glaze. The glaze allows the caramel wall color to peek through and creates a sheer, floating effect that complements the fabric.

guardian angel

A color palette of deep cranberry and yellow ocher turned a boxy bedroom into a sexy hideaway. Cherie had previously sponged her walls with these same colors, but the results were messy and uneven. Paint finishes like sponging and ragging are most successful when the base coat and the top coat are similar in tone and hue. I helped her to use the colors she loved in a more elegant way. The ceiling was antiqued in soothing tones of gold and mustard yellows like those found in French bistros (although those patinas are usually the results of years of tobacco smoke). I striped the walls with a visual trick called shadow striping. The wide stripes "lift" the low ceiling and the tone-on-tone sheen provides a luxurious backdrop to this couple's rich linens and collection of antique angels.

before

golden patina ceiling

MATERIALS AND TOOLS

low-tack painter's tape (optional)

white, light ocher, and dark ocher latex
paint, satin

roller and paint tray and extension
pole

double roller and paint tray (see
Colorworks in Resources)

satin acrylic varnish

3″ varnish brush or sponge roller

This is a fabulous solution for uneven, bumpy, and cracked ceilings. In contrast to a coat of flat white, which would show every mark, this patina will camouflage every flaw. The ceiling was cleaned and then base-coated in creamy white. I mixed two deep yellow glazes, one golden and the other more of a mustard hue. I used a divided, or double, roller and tray to apply the colored glazes to speed up the process. As the two colors blend together, a mixture of different tones of yellow appears. Once it was dry, I applied a coat of mid-sheen varnish. This sheen reflects the colors in the room, spreading a warm glow.

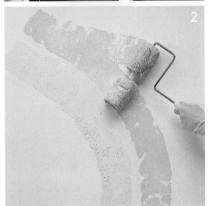

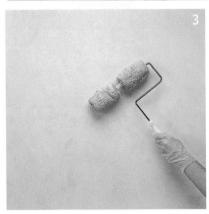

For best results, prepare your surface following the instructions in the preparation section, page 44.

step 1   To keep a neat edge between the ceiling and the walls, you may want to run tape along the top of the walls.

step 2   Apply 2 base coats of white to the ceiling and let dry. Use regular latex paint because ceiling paint is porous, and does not make a good base for a paint technique.

step 3   (*Shot 1*) In the divided paint tray, pour light ocher paint on one side and dark ocher paint on the other. Roll the divided roller through the colors to coat each side fully.

step 4   (*Shot 2*) Roll the paint onto the ceiling in wide arcs, going back and forth and covering the surface in broad strokes without removing the roller from the surface. Go over the area in different directions, getting rid of roller marks and blending the colors together. Do not overblend or the colors will become muddy.

step 5   (*Shot 3*) Stand back and look at your work. You can always add more paint to re-cover areas that are not blended well.

step 6   Varnish the ceiling to give it a glossy sheen.

shadow stripes

MATERIALS AND TOOLS

primer

burgundy latex paint, satin (or your color of choice)

mixing bucket

roller and paint tray

ruler and chalk

weighted chalk line (plumb line)

low-tack painter's tape

semi-gloss or high-gloss water-based varnish

3″ varnish brush or sponge roller

or high-gloss latex paint in same color

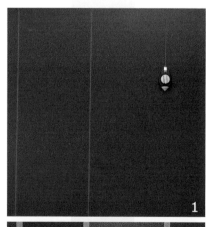

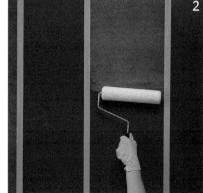

Shadow-striped wallpaper has been in vogue for generations as a formal and elegant wall treatment. A richer and more unique finish can be produced with paint at a fraction of the cost, and in the same time that it would take to hang the paper. It works best with elegant colors: Try rich cream, taupe, hunter green, cobalt blue, or, as we have here, a deep tone of cranberry. The walls are first base-coated in a low sheen of the chosen color, then measured and marked out for the vertical stripes. Every other stripe becomes a high-gloss sheen of the same color. There are two ways to achieve this. The first is to use a high-gloss sheen of the same color paint for the alternate stripe. The second method is to apply one coat of semi- or high-gloss varnish over each alternate stripe.

For best results, prepare your surface following the instructions in the preparation section, page 44.

step 1   Have the paint store tint the primer. This will make it easier to get good coverage with the dark paint color. Apply the tinted primer to the walls and let dry.

step 2   Apply at least 2 coats of satin sheen burgundy paint to the walls. Let dry completely. With dark colors it is sometimes necessary to add a third coat to achieve full coverage.

step 3   (Shot 1) Divide the walls into stripes; ours are 12″ wide. Mark every 12″ along the top of the walls with chalk, and use a weighted chalk line to mark off the vertical stripes.

step 4   (Shot 2) Tape off alternate stripes to be varnished or painted with high-gloss paint by running the tape along the outside of each stripe to be varnished. When you have finished taping, you will have thin and thick stripes. Apply the varnish to the thick stripes. It goes on milky and dries clear. Remove the tape.

bed canopy

Cherie had many angels that she had collected from all corners of the world. We took her largest cherub and attached it to a wood box with a large hook and eye. We made the 12″ × 14″ box from pine, and finished it to match the bedside tables, but instead of crackling the top with crackle varnish, we antiqued the piece by rubbing a thin burnt umber glaze over its surface with a soft rag. Voile was hung from the inside of the box, hooked over fleur-de-lis curtain stays, and draped behind the bed.

crackle table top

MATERIALS AND TOOLS

ocher, pale yellow, burnt orange and burnt umber latex paint, satin

3" paintbrush

water-based glazing liquid

3 mixing containers

2" paintbrush

soft, clean, lint-free rags

crackle varnish kit (available at craft stores)

burnt umber artist's oil

oil-based varnish (optional)

varnish brush or sponge roller

RECIPE

1 part latex paint

3 parts glazing liquid

step 1   Apply 2 base coats of ocher to cover the table and let dry for 4 hours.

step 2   (*Shot 1*) Mix the pale yellow, burnt orange and burnt umber glazes according to the recipe. Apply the pale yellow glaze loosely over the whole surface with a 3" brush.

step 3   (*Shot 2*) While the pale yellow is wet, dab on the burnt orange, then the burnt umber glazes randomly with a brush. Use a rag to gently blend the three colors, creating a mottled marble effect. Let dry overnight.

step 4   (*Shot 3*) Apply the two varnishes from the crackle kit following the directions found in the kit. The two varnishes don't like each other and cracks will appear as they dry. Let dry and cure overnight.

step 5   (*Shot 4*) Rub burnt umber artist's oil into the cracks and wipe the excess off with a rag.

Note: If you choose to varnish the top, use an oil-based varnish.

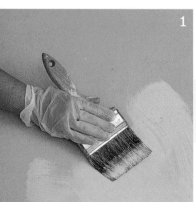

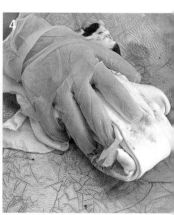

To complement the plaster angel holding up the canopy, I dressed up the side tables (flea market finds) with paper and an antique finish. I found an old calendar of historic paintings of angelic cherubs. The width of the calendar fit the dimensions of the drawers perfectly. I first applied a simple marble effect to the whole piece, then glued on the paper. The crackle varnishes were then applied to the top of the table. Once the varnishes have dried, hairline cracks appear that are almost invisible. When a small dab of burnt umber artist's oil is rubbed over the surface, the cracks immediately jump out, creating an authentic-looking antique finish.

french
country

A rural home in southern France is as simple as it is magical. Pure hues and natural colors combined with an eclectic mix of antiques and flea market finds are the basic elements. Unlike opulent Parisian interiors with their ornate plasterwork and richly paneled rooms, these country farms and villas have a quieter elegance. Plaster walls are washed in earth tones and floors are either wood or stone.

How is it possible to re-create this serenity in our own homes? This suburban home was built in the mid '80s with very little attention to detail. The bedroom ceiling is low with no moldings, and the lines of the room are plain. Instead of seeing this as a dilemma, we worked with the room's simplicity and took inspiration from the textures and hues of the homes in Provence.

before

provençal walls

Although these walls are standard drywall, I replicated the character of ancient plaster walls found in most French country interiors. Because there are no ceiling moldings, I introduced a simple detail by breaking up the walls into two contrasting colors. A delicate peach was rubbed over the surface of the upper half and a clay gray on the lower. I painted a band of charcoal to highlight the division between top and bottom. The technique of color washing is the easiest way to reproduce an uneven finish similar to the look of colors that have been broken down or faded by the sun and time.

UPPER WALL MATERIALS AND TOOLS

measuring tape

pencil

chalk line

low-tack painter's tape

cream, dark peach, and light peach
    latex paint, satin

roller and paint tray

water-based glazing liquid

mixing containers

2″ paintbrush

badger-hair or soft bristle brush

RECIPE

1 part latex paint

3 parts water-based glazing liquid

For best results, prepare your surface following the instructions in the preparation section, page 44.

step 1   Measure and tape off a line where the upper wall meets the dado. This is usually 3′–3½′ from the floor. Apply 2 base coats of cream to the upper wall and let dry for 4 hours.

step 2   (Shot 1) Mix the 2 peach-colored glazes according to the recipe. Working in 3′–4′ square sections, apply the darker glaze first, brushing in diagonal strokes randomly over the surface.

step 3   (Shot 2) Using the same brush, apply the paler glaze in the same diagonal strokes, filling in all the spaces around the darker strokes. Work quickly so the glaze will remain wet.

step 4   (Shot 3) Use the soft bristle brush to blend the colors together. Start by blending along the same diagonal, then just tickle the surface in different directions to soften the effect. Remove the tape and let dry overnight.

LOWER WALL OR DADO
MATERIALS AND TOOLS

low-tack painter's tape

medium gray, charcoal, and pale cream latex paint, satin

roller and paint tray

ruler

pencil

chalk line

small foam roller and paint tray

water-based glazing liquid

mixing container

wide paintbrush

rags or paper towel

step 1   Tape off the line between the upper and lower wall. Apply 2 base coats of medium gray to the lower wall and let dry overnight as you will be taping over it.

step 2   (*Shot 1*) One inch below the top of the dado, measure a 2"-wide stripe, then mark with a chalk line to ensure that it is straight. Run tape along the outside of the stripe lines. Fill in the stripe with charcoal paint. Remove the tape and let dry for 4 hours.

step 3   (*Shot 2*) Mix the cream glaze according to the recipe for upper walls. Dip a wide brush into the colored glaze and remove the excess onto a rag. Drag the bristles lightly over the dado's surface in vertical and horizontal directions. This dry-brush technique will give the dado a mottled look.

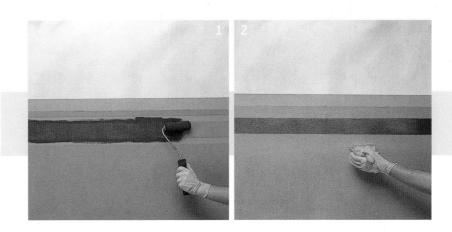

gingham
guest
room

If you have a room that gets plenty of natural light, design the space around this wonderful opportunity. Use translucent but bright colors for the walls and sheer fabrics that soften and diffuse the light. This guest room was a joy to decorate with the sunlight streaming through the French doors. A light green paint was mixed with glazing liquid to produce a delicate plaid design on the walls that looks like sheer gingham. The hardwood floors were painted the palest green and bordered with a stenciled floral swag. An antiqued iron daybed sits against the wall, draped by panels of sheer creamy cotton batiste that are gathered high on the wall over a brass rod. This is a beautiful guest room or a special place in your home where you can recharge your batteries.

before

gingham walls

A translucent checkered pattern was painted over all the bedroom walls using a light green glaze. If the checks had been applied in a solid color, they would have been extremely heavy, but instead the translucent finish keeps the room light and airy. The walls were first measured out into equal horizontal stripes. Use a chalk line and level (you will need two people for this), and then tape off the stripes. Once the colored glaze was applied, I pulled a hard bristle brush through the wet glaze, creating a soft dragged effect like the weave in fabric. The dragged horizontal stripes were left to dry overnight and then the vertical stripes were measured and painted the same way. Where the glazed stripes cross each other, the color is heavier, giving the illusion of a gingham pattern.

MATERIALS AND TOOLS

*bright off-white and light green latex
    paint, satin*

roller and paint tray

measuring tape

pencil

chalk line

low-tack painter's tape

water-based glazing liquid

mixing container

stiff bristle brush

RECIPE

1 part latex paint

3 parts water-based glazing liquid

1 part water

For best results, prepare your surface following the instructions in the preparation section, page 44.

step 1   Apply 2 base coats of white and let dry overnight.

step 2   (*Shot 1*) Decide on the width of your gingham stripes and mark off the horizontal lines with the chalk line.

step 3   (*Shot 2*) You will be painting alternate stripes, so apply tape to the *outside* of the stripes that need to be painted. When you are finished taping, these stripes will look wider. If it helps, tape an X on the stripes not to be painted—the thinner stripes. Mix the green-colored glaze according to the recipe. Roll the colored glaze onto alternate stripes.

step 4   (*Shot 3*) Using a stiff bristle brush, drag along the length of the painted stripe, horizontally only, to give the effect of a cloth weave. Go over it a couple of times, brushing and blending out any harsh marks. Let dry overnight.

step 5   (*Shot 4*) Mark off vertical stripes the same width as the horizontal stripes.

step 6   (*Shot 5*) Fill in alternate vertical stripes as you did for the horizontal stripes. This time, drag the bristle brush through vertically.

The hardwood floor was first stripped of any varnish and stain (see page 47) and primed with a water-based primer. I then applied two coats of light apple green and left the floor to cure overnight. The corner stencil was held in place with spray adhesive. Instead of using stencil paint and a stencil brush to paint the design, I used a small airbrush kit that made the job move along quickly. These are available from craft stores. Airbrush stenciling is not difficult, and produces a smoother effect than traditional stenciling. The colors blend together as they are "misted" onto the surface.

MATERIALS AND TOOLS

low-tack painter's tape

high-adhesion primer

3″ paintbrush

roller with an extension pole and paint tray

pale apple green, and gray/blue latex paint, satin

ruler

chalk line

1″ paintbrush

paper towel

airbrush kit

bucket of water

drop cloth

newspaper or craft paper

stencil

spray adhesive

green, burnt sienna, and yellow latex paint, satin

face mask

acrylic varnish

foam roller

For best results, prepare your surface following the instructions in the preparation section, page 44.

step 1   (*Shot 1*) Once the floor is sanded and clean, tape off the quarter-round molding to protect it from paint. Prime the floor, using the 3″ paintbrush to get into the corners and edges, and then the extension pole on the roller for the rest of the job. Let dry overnight. Apply 2 base coats of pale green and let dry overnight.

step 2   (*Shot 2*) With a ruler and chalk line, measure and mark off a 1½″ border around the floor about 10″ inches in from the wall. Tape off the border with the low-tack tape. Fill in the border with gray/blue paint using the 1″ paintbrush.

step 3   Set up the airbrush tool following the instructions that come with it. Water down the latex paint or it will clog the nozzle. When you change colors, dip the sprayer into a bucket of water to clean it. Use the drop cloth and newspaper to cover up all nearby surfaces, as spray paint becomes airborne.

step 4   (*Shot 3*) Spray the back of the stencil with adhesive and press it down into position on the floor. Cover all parts of the stencil with newspaper except the section you are spraying. Wearing a face mask and working in a well-ventilated area, hold the sprayer about a foot above the surface and spray lightly back and forth, building up the color. When you change colors, remember to cover up the part you just painted. Lift the stencil and let dry.

step 5   Apply 4 coats of acrylic varnish to the floor. Let the floor dry and cure for a week before moving furniture back into the room.

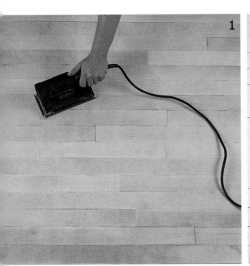
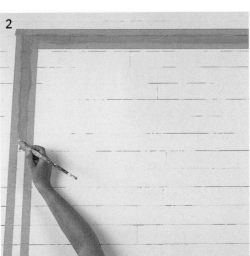
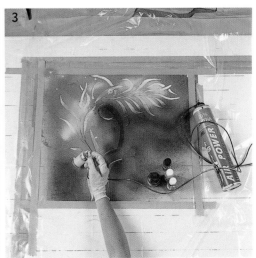

grand opera

Marco and Donna have a vast bedroom with a curved ceiling. It's not often that you are awarded such a dramatic space to design, so I took full advantage. I had previously visited a very special hotel in Italy called Palazzo Terranova (see page 33). It's a large villa sitting high up in the Umbrian hills in the heart of Italy. Tuscan and Umbrian homes rarely have moldings or trim work, so artisans paint detail directly onto the walls. As you see in the complex frescoes that adorn many buildings, these artisans also rub the local earthy colors directly onto the walls, and use a technique called "lining" to add detail. These slim lines are usually hand-painted to finish off a rubbed or color-washed wall. At Palazzo Terranova the walls were also high, so they were brought down to scale by creating a painted fringe around the ceiling. We adopted this inventive idea in Marco and Donna's bedroom and added painted swags over the slope of the ceiling. The highlight of the room is the painted headboard. The most difficult part of the project is making the stencil for the wrought iron, but it is worth the time as the results are stunning.

before

painted ceiling swag and tassels

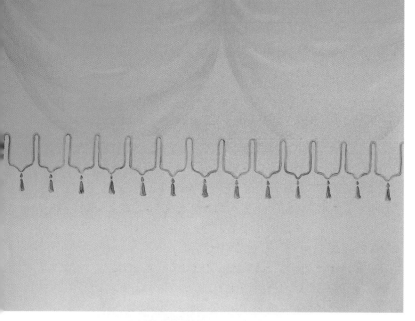

For the ceiling, I chose a palette of rich earthy ochers and golden yellow over a cream base coat. A golden yellow glaze was rubbed to age the surface. Once the ceiling was dry, we painted simple swags to give the illusion of softly gathered fabric. This "fabric" was finished with a stenciled fringe and tassels. You can make a stencil to fit the proportions of your room by cutting out a series of the same design along a piece of Mylar. To speed up the painting process, use a roller to fill in the fringe. The tassels are stenciled on one at a time, positioned at the center of each section of fringe.

For best results prepare your surface following the instructions in the preparation section, page 44.

Note: In the bedroom, the faux swagged fabric is painted over the curved section of the ceiling behind the bed, and continued around the flat upper walls. The dentil and tassel are painted underneath the fabric over the veiled walls (see page 127 for veiling). We have photographed these instructions on a flat wall. The upper 20" border is golden yellow, and the main wall is veiled. Low-tack painter's tape masks off the line between the border and the veiled wall.

step 1   (*Shot 1*) Measure and divide the area to be swagged into 30" widths. Tape string down to divide the panels, and check with a level that the string is hanging straight.

step 2   (*Shot 2*) Mix the 3 yellow glazes. Roll the golden yellow glaze over the first 30" section. This will give a slippery surface for blending the other glazes.

MATERIALS AND TOOLS

measuring tape

pencil

string or embroidery thread

low-tack painter's tape

level

light yellow, golden yellow, and dark yellow latex paint, satin

water-based glazing liquid

mixing containers

2 small foam rollers and paint trays

two ½" artist's brushes

1" paintbrush

dentil stencil or Mylar, marker, and X-acto knife

spray adhesive

indigo blue artist's acrylic

tassel stencil (see Resources)

RECIPE

1 part latex paint

2 to 3 parts water-based glazing liquid

step 3 (*Shot 3*) Dip an artist's brush into the darker yellow glaze. Find the center of the section and draw a simple Christmas tree shape down the center. The lines do not need to be symmetrical, but they should join with the lines that are to be drawn in the areas on either side. These lines will form the shadows of the folds of the drapery. The line nearest the bottom should disappear into the corner.

step 4 (*Shot 4*) Dip another artist's brush into the lightest yellow glaze. Brush the glaze on just above the dark branches you have just applied.

step 5 Dip a 1″ paintbrush into the golden yellow glaze and blend it softly through the light and dark lines to even out the shading. Make sure you go slightly under the string so that the fabric panels will be joined. Let dry for 4 hours.

step 6 (*Shot 5*) You can buy a dentil stencil, or it is easy to make one. Draw the shape onto a piece of paper, then trace it onto a strip of Mylar. Move the paper along and repeat the design so that you have 4 or 5 in a row. Cut out the stencil with a sharp knife. Spray the back of the dentil stencil with adhesive and position it under the swagged "fabric." Use a roller and the golden yellow paint to fill in the stencil. Roll most of the paint off the roller so you won't leak under the stencil. Remove the stencil and reposition along the faux fabric until you are finished but don't reposition over an area until the previous stenciled dentil is dry, or you will smudge the paint. Let dry for 4 hours.

step 7 (*Shot 6*) Mix the indigo blue artist's acrylic with a little glaze and outline the dentils using an artist's brush.

step 8 (*Shot 7*) Use spray adhesive to center the tassel stencil under each dentil. Fill in the stencil with the blue acrylic paint on an artist's brush to give it a more freehand look.

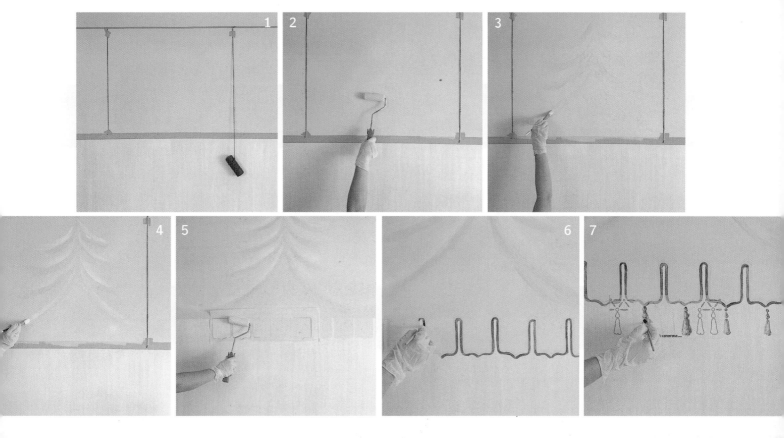

faux wrought-iron headboard

This project takes some patience, but the effect is unbelievable. First sketch out the pattern that you want for the faux iron headboard. Once you are happy with the design, enlarge it on a photocopier until the proportions fit the size and dimensions of your bed. You need to make a stencil for only half the design. Because this is a king-sized bed, we made the stencil repeat four times. The finished design looks like twin beds pushed together. As an added touch, each side has Donna's or Marco's initials stenciled onto it, but this was done at the end. When you are cutting a stencil with an intricate pattern, you will need to cut bridges to prevent the centers of the stencil from falling out. Mark the wall exactly where you want the bed and the headboard to be. The stenciling itself is fast, but make sure your pencil registration marks are accurate. The key to a realistic faux headboard is to fill in shadow lines. The shadow is stenciled first using the same stencil, and then the stencil is moved an inch up and to the right for the wrought iron. Once the first half of the twin bed is stenciled, clean and dry the back of the stencil carefully. Now flip it over so you have the reverse image butted up against the first image, and repeat the same process. For a king-sized bed, repeat a second twin bed headboard right beside the first one. The illusion is astonishing.

MATERIALS AND TOOLS

measuring tape

pencil

headboard stencil

spray adhesive

low-tack painter's tape

*medium gray and black latex or stencil
    paint*

paper plates

2 stencil brushes

paper towels

small artist's brush

faux wrought-iron headboard continued

For best results, prepare your surface following the instructions in the preparation section, page 44.

step 1   With a measuring tape and pencil, measure and mark where the stencil is going to go on the wall.

step 2   (*Shot 1*) The same stencil is used for the faux wrought-iron outline and its shadow. Fill in the shadow lines first. Spray the back of the stencil with adhesive, and place the stencil 1″ down and 1″ to the right of the position marked for the wrought-iron stencil. Pour gray paint onto a plate, and dip a stencil brush into the paint. Wipe off the excess paint by swirling the brush around on a paper towel. Fill in the stencil with swirling or pouncing motions. Remove the stencil and clean it. Fill in the bridges with gray paint and an artist's brush.

step 3   (*Shot 2*) When the gray shadow is dry, position the stencil in its originally marked position, 1″ up and 1″ to the left of the shadow line. Stencil with black as you did with gray. Remove the stencil and let dry.

step 4   (*Shot 3*) Use the artist's brush and black paint to fill in the bridge gaps.

veiled walls

MATERIALS AND TOOLS

white latex paint, satin
bucket of water
4"–6"-wide bristle brush

The bedroom walls were a golden yellow, and the ceiling creamy white. I decided to reverse the color scheme, and softened the walls with a veiled paint effect. Over the existing yellow base coat, I used a wide bristle brush to apply white latex paint thinned down with water. I brushed vertically, pulling through the paint wash until the surface took on the appearance of soft sheer fabric with the yellow gently peeking through.

For best results, prepare your surface following the instructions in the preparation section, page 44.

The walls in this bedroom have a yellow base coat.

step 1   (*Shot 1*) Dip a wide brush into white paint, and then dip it into water. Apply the paint to the wall in long vertical strokes. If the paint doesn't move very well on the wall, dip the brush into the water again to make it runnier.

step 2   Go over the area as many times as you like until you get a smoky weave effect.

wood
and
whimsy

The bedroom in this loft was a bright open space, but it had very little character. Barbara had just moved away from home, and found there was not much money left over for furnishings. We decided to keep the bedroom light and uncluttered. Barbara purchased a queen-sized bed frame and mattress to which we attached industrial-sized wheels. This immediately made the bed contemporary. Over the last few years there has been a trend toward overscale furniture, huge sofas, giant lampshades, and big tall headboards. Rather than spending money on an expensive headboard, I painted one directly onto the wall; its clean modern shape replicates the look of blond wood. The faux wood theme was repeated on the bi-fold cupboard doors. The honey color of the painted wood and the new linens become accents of warmth and contrast in the large modern space.

burled wood
cupboard doors

MATERIALS AND TOOLS

cream latex paint, satin

small roller and tray

face mask

stout beer

rubbing alcohol

*burnt umber and burnt sienna powder
  pigment*

measuring spoon

mixing container

1″ artist's brush

soft, clean, lint-free rags

fine, pointed artist's brush

low-sheen acrylic spray varnish

RECIPE

³/₄ cup beer

¹/₂ cup rubbing alcohol

1 tablespoon burnt umber powder

¹/₂ tablespoon burnt sienna powder

Bi-fold doors are probably the most common bedroom cupboard doors around. Although they are rather plain and boring, their flat surface is ideal for painting and decorating. The cupboard in this contemporary bedroom has been painted to resemble blond burled walnut. I used the same glaze recipe for the door as I did for the Faux Wood Headboard on page 133. The tones are the same, but this wood has a mottled rather than grainy appearance.

For best results prepare your surface following the instructions in the preparation section, page 44.

step 1   Apply 2 base coats of cream and let dry for 4 hours.

step 2   Put on a face mask and mix the glaze according to the recipe. Always wear a mask when working with powdered pigments because they become airborne and are toxic.

step 3   (*Shots 1 and 2*) Swirl the glaze over the surface with a 1″ artist's brush and a rag. You want a soft, mottled circular effect. Let dry for 2 to 4 hours.

step 4   (*Shot 3*) Dip the fine artist's brush into the glaze and
make tiny circular grain lines following some of the
lines that have been formed from the mottling. These
lines should never be straight. Roll the brush around
on the surface. Add little dots around the lines to
make the bird's eyes. Let dry overnight.

step 5   You must use spray varnish to seal and protect. If you
brush varnish over this glaze, it will remove your
effect. After spraying 2 coats, if you want more protection, you may continue with a liquid varnish and
sponge brush. Always wear a mask when spraying, and
cover up anything you don't want varnished as the
spray is airborne. Work in a well-ventilated area. Wait
24 to 48 hours for the final coat of varnish to cure.

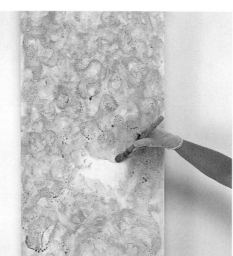
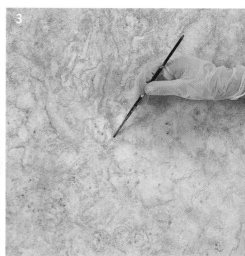

faux wood headboard

measuring tape

ruler

pencil

low-tack painter's tape

deep cream latex paint, satin

small roller and tray

face mask

stout beer

rubbing alcohol

*burnt umber and burnt sienna powder
    pigment*

measuring spoon

mixing container

2″ paintbrush

soft, clean, lint-free rags

badger-hair or soft bristle brush

thin, pointed artist's brush

*a small amount of brown/gray latex or
    artist's acrylic paint*

satin acrylic spray varnish

RECIPE

³/₄ cup beer

½ cup rubbing alcohol

1 tablespoon burnt umber powder

½ tablespoon burnt sienna powder

Oversized furniture is an enormous trend in home design. The bigger-is-better appeal is a winning complement to open plan rooms with ceilings that soar. These big pieces could also fit into an average-size room—as long as there is little else to fight for space. This faux wood headboard is painted in two pieces because you would not get real wood this wide. Instead of using a standard glazing liquid, I mixed paint with rubbing alcohol and beer. The glaze is very translucent, illustrating the delicate finish found in light woods. Honey blond is an easy color to live with, perfect for the clean, contemporary lines of our faux headboard.

Before you start painting, set up your bedroom furniture including the position of the bed, as a painted headboard cannot be moved!

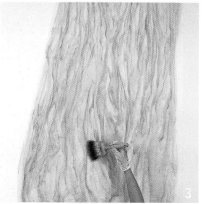

For best results, prepare your surface following the instructions in the preparation section, page 44.

step 1   Measure and mark the outline for the headboard on the wall with a pencil. Tape off around the outside of the pencil marks, and apply 2 base coats of dark cream. Let dry for 4 hours.

step 2   Run a piece of tape down the middle of the headboard, and work on one side at a time.

step 3   (Shot 1) Put on a face mask and mix the glaze according to the recipe. Always wear a mask when working with powdered pigments because they become airborne and are toxic.

step 4   (Shot 2) Dip a 2″ paintbrush into the glaze and apply it to the surface in jagged lines, leaving darker and lighter lines and spaces. Fold up a soft rag and dab over the wet glaze to soften. Push the paint around with the brush to create grain lines. Always move in the same direction.

step 5   (Shot 3) Brush the soft bristle brush very gently over the surface to soften the lines, but don't erase them. Always move in the direction of the grain.

step 6   (Shot 4) To make knots, look for areas in the faux grain where they would occur naturally. Dip the artist's brush in the glaze and make little irregular circles with lines coming out along the grain. (Look at a piece of real wood for accuracy.)

step 7   Let dry for 4 hours. Retape on the finished side of the headboard and repeat the technique on the second side. Let dry.

step 8   (Shot 5) Remove the tape and apply a shadow line down the side of the headboard with brown/gray paint. Mask it off to ensure a straight edge. The shadow starts off about 1″ thick and gradually increases to 3″.

step 9   You must use spray varnish to seal and protect this surface. If you brush varnish over this glaze, it will remove your effect. After spraying 2 coats, you may continue with a brush. Always wear a mask when spraying, and cover up anything you don't want varnished as the spray is airborne. Work in a well-ventilated area. Wait 24 to 48 hours for final coat of varnish to cure.

earthy origins

Warm earthy tones range from the red/brown of an African landscape to vibrant oranges, from yellow ochers to the cool pink of wet plaster. Earth colors are naturally compatible with all surroundings, and are as at home in a modern interior as a country setting. As paint colors, they translate best when they are textured onto walls. Straight from the can with a roller, the colors can be harsh, but when rubbed over a pale base coat, the light bounces dramatically back into the room. The selection of terra-cottas in commercial house paints tends to be flat and dull, and shares none of the vibrancy of these real earth pigments, which can be created by using artist's acrylics or powdered pigments. Try mixing burnt sienna, burnt umber, yellow ocher, or raw umber with a glaze and you will discover the subtlety and beauty of this natural palette.

This small bedside table was bought as raw furniture—it had no paint or stain. We added our own design. The top of the table was first painted black and the legs white. Once dry, the top was painted white, with gray on the drawer front and the legs. After leaving the piece to dry overnight, I took medium-grain sandpaper and rubbed the top layer of paint off in random areas to reveal the base coat. The table was finished with a gold trim around the edge of the top. An inexpensive new table has now become a timeless piece worn with age.

antiqued walls

These walls remind us of the baking heat of a Tuscan summer or lazy afternoons in a Mexican village. Their warmth and vibrancy are cooled down with fresh white linens. The texture of the walls is rough and uneven to create the illusion of old faded walls and peeling paint. A colored glaze was made by mixing burnt sienna, ocher, and raw umber artist's acrylics into water-based glazing liquid. Apply the glaze with a roller and while it is still wet, lay a wet cheesecloth over the surface. Leave areas of color that are heavier than others, and areas where more base coat is seen. It's best if you work in areas of 4 square feet at one time.

MATERIALS AND TOOLS

cream latex paint, satin

roller and paint tray

burnt sienna, ocher, and raw umber artist's acrylics

water-based glazing liquid

mixing container

soft, clean, lint-free rags or cheesecloth

bucket of water

latex gloves

RECIPE

1 tablespoon burnt sienna artist's acrylic

$^1/_2$ tablespoon ocher artist's acrylic

1 teaspoon raw umber artist's acrylic

3 cups glazing liquid

$1^1/_2$ cups water

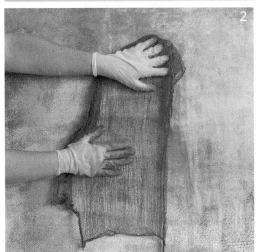

For best results, prepare your surface following the instructions in the preparation section, page 44.

step 1   Apply 2 base coats of cream and let dry for 4 hours.

step 2   (Shot 1) Mix the colored glaze according to the recipe. Working in 4' sections, roll on the glaze in vertical and horizontal strokes. Make some patches of color heavier than others; you don't want an opaque surface.

step 3   (Shot 2) Soak a rag or cheesecloth in water, squeeze it out, and then soak it in the glaze. Wearing gloves, squeeze it so that it is not dripping, then unfold it and lay it on the wall. Press it down lightly with your gloved hand. Continue this technique randomly over the glazed wall. Fold the rag and use it to blend any roller marks or fingerprints. Do not blend away the overall weave pattern. Rinse the rag in water and squeeze it out. Dab in various areas to lighten patches.

step 4   Move onto the next section, keeping a wet edge (see page 58).

italian style

In the chapter on hotel bedrooms from around the world I spoke of one of my favorite places on this planet: a jewel in the heart of Italy called Palazzo Terranova. The whole villa has an ancient sun-drenched ambience. The walls in each guest room are painted with colors taken from the surrounding landscapes. Earthy terra-cottas, burnt umbers and yellow ochers are mixed with the vibrant tones of the local fruits and vegetables. There are colorwashes taken from the most delicate herbs and spices such as lavender and mustard, sage and cornflower. The use of color in this magical place makes your heart sing. It's not only the unusual combinations of colors, but also the simplicity of their application that renders them so easy to adapt to our own homes. The lively panels in this bedroom will make a room look cheerful and welcoming. You may not have a beamed ceiling, but the walls alone will make any bedroom special. The furnishings are a combination of local finds and hand-painted pieces.

painted panel walls

MATERIALS AND TOOLS

*pale bright yellow, white, ocher, and
    dusty pink latex paint, satin*

roller and paint tray

measuring tape

pencil

long metal ruler

plumb line

chalk line

1"-wide low-tack painter's tape

small foam rollers and paint trays

water-based glazing liquid

mixing containers

3" stiff bristle brush

soft, clean, lint-free rags

badger-hair or soft bristle brush

charcoal watercolor pencil

RECIPES FOR OCHER AND PINK GLAZES

1 part latex paint

2 parts water-based glazing liquid

1 part water

FOR WHITE GLAZE

1 part latex paint

2 parts water-based glazing liquid

2 parts water

I copied the look of the painted panels I saw in one of the bedrooms at Palazzo Terranova. Vertical panels will always make rooms look higher as they draw the eye upward. Fat rectangles were marked and taped over a pale bright yellow base coat and filled in alternately with ocher and pink glazes. Before the tape was removed, I added a final coat of thin white glaze over all the panels to soften the colors. When the surface was dry, I removed the tape and drew in highlight lines around each panel with a charcoal watercolor pencil.

For best results prepare your surface following the instructions in the preparation section, page 44.

step 1 Apply 2 base coats of pale bright yellow and let dry overnight.

step 2 Using a pencil and long ruler, plumb line, and chalk line, divide the walls into panels. From the floor the panels run vertically approximately 15" wide and 75" high; then create panels that run horizontally on top of these. The horizontal panels run the width of 3 vertical panels 15" high and 45" wide. Use 1" low-tack painter's tape to tape off the panels. Apply the tape over the chalk lines. The bright yellow base coat will frame the panels.

step 3 (Shot 1) Paint every second panel white.

step 4 (Shot 2) Mix the ocher and pink glazes. With a 3" paintbrush, apply the ocher glaze over the vertical and horizontal panels that are not white. Working on one panel at a time, brush on the glaze in the direction the panel runs.

step 5   *(Shot 3)* Dab the glaze with a soft rag to remove any obvious brush marks.

step 6   *(Shot 4)* Use the soft bristle brush to blend and soften the glaze.

step 7   *(Shot 5)* Apply the pink glaze over the dry white painted panels following the same technique in steps 3 through 5. Do not remove the tape yet. Let dry overnight.

step 8   Mix the white glaze and apply it over the entire wall surface, again using a rag and softening brush to blend and get rid of any brush marks. Work in patches about 4′ × 4′ and keep a wet edge (see page 58). The effect should be soft and cloudy. Remove the tape.

step 9   *(Shot 6)* With a long metal ruler and charcoal water-color pencil, outline all the panels.

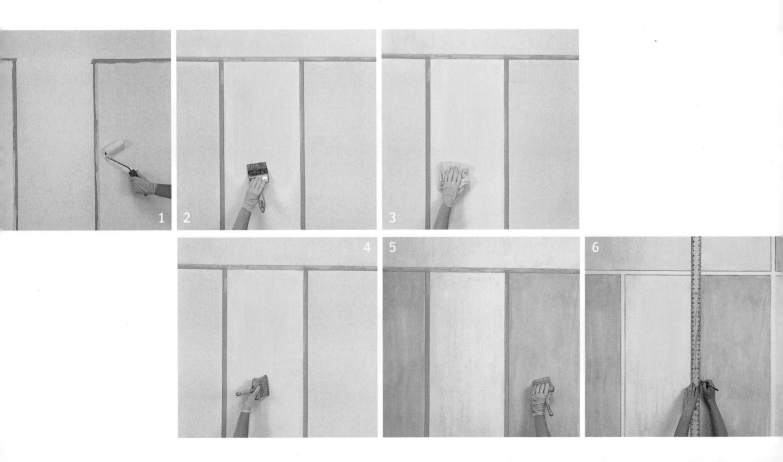

beamed ceiling

Beamed ceilings will always make a room unique. Found throughout Europe, they are often a featured element in Spanish-style houses in the United States. But, instead of painting the wood beams, why not paint the ceiling space in between? Here the pink and yellow and a dark chocolate are painted in geometric shapes.

handmade headboard

This headboard can be made from medium-density fiberboard or good quality plywood. After drawing out the design, cut the shape with a jigsaw. The bedposts are actually newel posts found at the hardware store. The charm of the bed is achieved by hand-painting a naïve design on the headboard and around the posts.

something old, something new

old door headboard

Rachel's original plan was to buy a new bed for her condominium bedroom. When she sought out my help, I thought it preferable to make a headboard from flea market finds, and then splurge on high-quality linens. We hit the jackpot on our second weekend of hunting—an old solid pine door. The panels were equally sized and spaced, and the door's height was the same as the width of a queen-size bed. Once the old paint was removed, we built up the height of the headboard by attaching a piece of medium-density fiberboard (MDF) and a crown molding. The flatness of the MDF was disguised by applying a length of Anaglypta, an embossed wallpaper border. These three different surfaces were then unified with 2 coats of cream paint. A brown glaze was rubbed over the entire piece to highlight the pattern on the Anaglypta, the textures on the panels of the old door, and the shape of the crown molding. Two pieces of 2″ × 2″ pine were attached to the back as legs and then the whole structure was secured to the wall with brackets.

parisian boudoir

For as long as she can remember, my friend Andrea has loved all things French. She revels in the magical sights and sounds of Paris and asked me to help her re-create the colors and elegant sensibilities of French decorating in her home. The bedroom walls are high but plain, so I had a blank canvas to work on. I added a cove molding around the top of the walls and then chose a creamy mustard color, a warm and welcoming yellow. The French love to dress up their walls with paneling and ornate moldings. I added these using paint, stencils, and shading to give dimension to the design. Panel frames were taped off and painted, then a watery coat of white paint was brushed over the whole wall and then repeated inside each panel to produce the textured look of fine linen. I continued to add detail by stenciling a beautiful design at the top of each panel, but instead of paint, the motif was filled in with water-soluble colored pencils. There were many steps involved in completing these gorgeous walls, but they transformed a plain space into an elegant boudoir, perfect for indulging the senses.

walls with a french twist

MATERIAL AND TOOLS

- sunny yellow, white, and pale blue latex paint, satin
- roller and paint tray
- ruler
- pencil
- plumb line
- level
- border frame stencil
- low-tack painter's tape
- 3" foam roller and paint tray
- stencil brush
- water-based glazing liquid
- water
- mixing container
- 3" paintbrush
- clean lint-free rags

RECIPE

- 1 part white latex paint
- 1 part water-based glazing liquid
- 3 to 4 parts water

A warm yellow is the base coat for these Parisian paneled walls. Once the panels were marked off, a corner stencil was used to make it easier to paint in neat curved corners. A thin layer of watered-down white paint was then applied to the walls to subdue the yellow slightly and integrate the overall pattern. This veiling technique was repeated inside the panels so they would stand out. The ornate stenciled motif at the top of each panel imitates the look of an intricately cut wood molding, and is called *faux boiserie*. After filling in the stenciled image with three shades of water-soluble colored pencils, water was brushed on to blend the colors.

step 1   Apply two base coats of yellow paint and let dry for 4 hours or overnight.

step 2   Use the ruler, pencil, and plumb line to measure and divide the wall into panels, alternating between two-foot and three-foot-wide panels. Leave about 6" above and below the panels. Check that all the lines are straight with the level.

step 3   (*Shot 1*) Place the border frame stencil in the corners of each of the frames and mark the edges. Mask off each panel's straight lines. Fill in the border frame with the small roller and white paint. Let dry for 4 hours.

step 4   (*Shot 2*) Our border stencil also has a cutout for shadow lines. Line up the stencil so that the shadow line sits against one edge of the frame. Dip the stencil brush into the pale blue paint, remove the excess on a paper towel or rag, and swirl the stencil brush over the cutout line. Move the stencil along the frame and continue the line. Make the shadow lines on the same side of each vertical panel frame, and at the bottom of the horizontals. Let dry for 4 hours.

step 5   (*Shot 3*) Mix the white glaze according to the recipe. It should be very runny, like milk. Dip the 3" brush into the glaze and brush up and down over the wall. Brush

in only one direction, vertically. The effect should be a very light veil of white. There will be visible brush marks. Let dry.

step 6   (Shot 4) Do a second veil coat inside the panels. Let dry.

faux boiserie

MATERIALS AND TOOLS

ruler

pencil

decorative stencil that will fit inside the panels (we used two stencils, one repeats in the large panels, and the other for the smaller panels)

low-tack painter's tape

brown, ocher and gray watercolor pencils

artist's brush

water

satin spray acrylic varnish (optional)

step 1   (Shot 1) Mark and make a note of the position of the stencil on the panel so you can repeat it in the other panels. Tape the stencil into place at the top of the first panel. Draw in the outline of the image using a pencil. Remove the stencil.

step 2   Color in the image with the watercolor pencils, using the gray for shadow, the yellow for highlights and the brown for the centers. The color does not have to be dark.

step 3   (Shot 2) Dip the artist's brush into water and go over the colored areas in strokes as long as possible. The water reacts with the water-soluble pencils and gives the ornamentation a painted watercolor look. Let dry.

step 4   Protect the watercolor stenciling with spray acrylic varnish. Varnish applied with a brush will wipe off your work. Oil-based varnish will discolor the white.

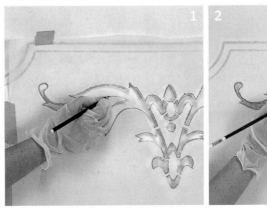
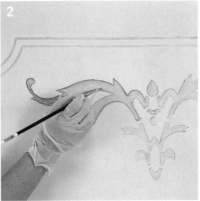

151

all spruced up

Aaron desperately needed some help with his bedroom. His goal was a masculine room that would reflect his bachelor lifestyle. I loved his choice of bed, but some of his accessories, especially the tourist-style fan above the bed, were a little over the top. His first attempt at decorating was fine, but the clean modern look that he had strived for was just not there yet. Aaron is a young radio broadcaster, so my vision was to design a room that reflected a more contemporary spirit. Inspired by the clean linear forms of a Norwegian sauna, we created the look of cedar plank walls with paint. The honey-colored faux wood worked well with the existing navy carpeting, and we matched up the blue on the ceiling. The sleigh bed was slipcovered in a cream canvas cloth to modernize the look. Floating shelves are not only practical, but add to the clean lines of the room. Although the room is sleek, there is a new twist to this modern style: it's also warm and cozy.

cedar walls

MATERIALS AND TOOLS

cream latex paint, satin

roller and paint tray

pencil

ruler

level

low-tack painter's tape

4" stiff bristle brush

*yellow brown and dark brown latex
    paint, satin*

water-based varnish, satin

3 mixing containers

soft, clean, lint-free rags

tan marker

RECIPE

1 part latex paint

4 parts water-based varnish

Inspired by a Swedish sauna, these walls radiate a seductive warmth. It looks complicated and time consuming to imitate wood planks with paint, but once you get into a rhythm it moves along quickly. The planks are marked off in varying lengths over a cream base coat. Instead of mixing paint with glazing liquid, we tinted varnish to the colors found in cedar. This adds a realistic sheen to the wood in one step. Apply both paint-tinted varnishes at the same time and run the brush through them to blend the colors together. As each plank is done separately, they'll all be slightly different. I used a marker and a ruler to highlight the edges of each plank.

step 1 Apply 2 base coats of cream and let dry for 4 hours.

step 2 (*Shot 1*) Measure and draw 6" wide planks along the wall, all irregular lengths. Use the level to make sure they run straight.

step 3 (*Shot 2*) Tape off along the outside of every other plank. Mix the yellow brown and dark brown glazes. Have a third container with water. Dip the brush into the water, then into the yellow brown glaze. Remove the excess onto a rag and pull along the length of the plank in one fluid movement. To make it look realistic, the grain in some planks will be straight and others wavy. The color will vary as well.

step 4 (*Shot 3*) Dip the brush into the darker glaze and remove the excess onto a rag. Add little waves to give more color variation. Every plank will look different just as in real wood. Go over your work until you are satisfied. If it dries before you are finished, brush on some water to open it up again.

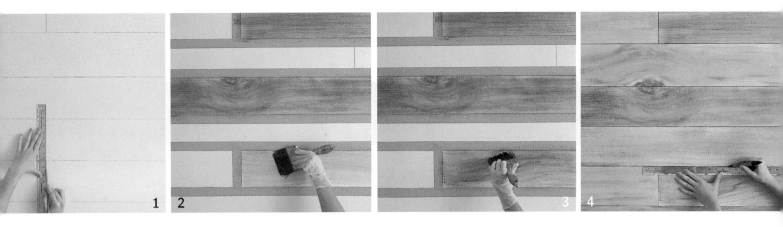

1 2 3 4

step 5   Remove the tape and let the finished planks dry for at
least 4 hours or overnight. Use the low-tack tape to tape
around the rest of the planks and paint them. Remove
the tape and leave to dry for 4 hours.

step 6   (*Shot 4*) Use the tan marker and draw along the pencil
lines to give depth to the planks resembling a beveled
edge.

corner detail

To make the outside corners look as if real boards
were used, on one wall I taped off an inch (the thickness of a plank) on every other board, painted in a
line along the tape with the tan marker, and stippled
over the colored glaze to resemble the look of the cut
end of a wooden plank. This step was repeated on the
other side of the corner, filling in the alternate
planks.

silvered shelf

Floating shelves are very popular if you want a modern, uncluttered look, as the hanging-bracket hardware is concealed within the shelves. They are practical above a bed since they don't jut out too far. These were only available in a white finish, so to add a little punch to the room, I enhanced them with a rough silver effect. I applied silver foil over a burgundy base coat. To get a more textured surface I laid a piece of burlap on top of the foil and rubbed over it with a roller. The effect of broken-up silver leaf with the burgundy showing through is interesting and contemporary. Because the underside of the shelf will be clearly visible from the bed, the silvered effect is applied to the top and bottom.

MATERIALS AND TOOLS

floating shelf the length of your headboard

burgundy latex paint, satin

2" paintbrush or small roller

aquasize (see Resources)

foam brush

silver transfer foil

piece of burlap long enough to cover shelf

small rubber roller

acrylic varnish, semi-gloss

Note: Work on the top and sides of the shelf first, and when the effect is complete, turn the shelf over and repeat on the underside.

step 1   Apply 2 base coats of burgundy to the shelf and let dry for 4 hours.

step 2   (Shot 1) Apply 2 coats of aquasize to the top and sides of the shelf with the foam roller. Let dry until it is clear and sticky.

step 3   (Shot 2) Lay the foil, shiny side up, flat on the shelf. Use the back of your hand to softly smooth it out.

step 4   (Shot 3) Lay a piece of burlap over the top of the foil and press down firmly over the burlap with the roller.

step 5   (Shot 4) Remove the burlap and the foil backing. If not enough of the foil has transferred, reapply by adding more aquasize and repeating steps 2 to 4.

step 6   Apply 3 coats of varnish for protection.

1 2 3 4

grommet curtains

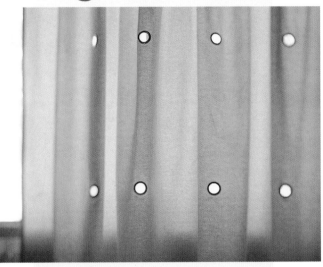

Canvas curtains were hung not just over the window area, but to cover the entire wall. Plain canvas was dressed up with a regular pattern of holes secured with steel grommets. The effect is not only stunning, but produces a beautiful soft pattern as the light flows into the room. To add to the modern feel of the room, we put these curtains on remote control so Aaron can open or close them from the bed.

MATERIALS AND TOOLS

cotton curtain panels
pencil
ruler
scissors
large plastic grommets, silver coated

step 1　Measure out and mark where you want the grommets to go. We put them in a straight grid, approximately every 24 inches.

step 2　(Shot 1) Cut a hole slightly smaller than the grommet at each marked spot.

step 3　(Shot 2) With one side of the grommet under the hole and the other over the hole, snap the grommet on, making sure to catch the fabric in the plastic teeth. They snap on easily.

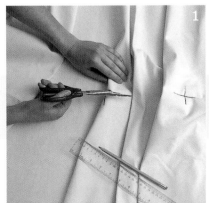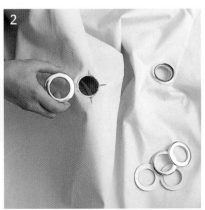

1 2

urban sleek

The words minimalist and modern do not usually evoke visions of comfort and warmth.
But sleek can be sensuous. Tones of black, gray, and white, when combined, will achieve a palette that is both sexy and sophisticated. This was the desired style for this contemporary bedroom—no frills or fuss. The decorating process began by purchasing a sleigh bed upholstered in clay-colored suede. But it is the wall behind the bed that creates a modern masculine touch. It becomes an architectural focal point by first cutting pieces of plywood to fit over a large area behind the bed, and then adding a grid of molding strips. These can be applied straight onto the drywall, but the plywood allows for an interesting dimension and texture. Paint the plywood and molding in the glossiest and darkest charcoal, a color that dances in daylight and is deeply dramatic in the evening.

two 4′ × 8′ sheeets of plywood, good
    one side

4 flat brackets and screws

primer

2 rollers and paint trays

medium- and fine-grade sandpaper

charcoal latex paint, high-gloss

chalk line

long ruler

½″ square molding, approximately
    ten 8′ strips

hand saw

right-angled ruler or set square

finishing nails

hammer

nail set

wood filler

½″ artist's brush

screws

screwdriver

Plywood is available in several different finishes and the quality of the wood varies greatly. For this large paneled wall we are using plywood to give the depth of a traditionally paneled room. You will need 2 sheets of 4′ × 8′ plywood that are smooth to the touch. It's best to paint the plywood and trim on the floor and then mount it on the wall with screws. The line where the sheets meet will fall underneath the pattern of grid lines. This oversized headboard is a very contemporary look.

step 1   (Shot 1) Attach the plywood sheets together from the back with brackets so that you have an 8′ square. Prime the plywood and molding strips. Let dry for 4 hours, and sand lightly.

step 2   Apply 2 base coats of the charcoal gloss paint to the plywood and molding and let dry for 4 hours.

step 3   (Shot 2) Divide the 8′ board into 2′ squares with the chalk line. You will have 16 squares. Using the set square for accuracy, line up and cut the molding strips to cover the lines. Nail the molding into place. Also nail molding strips around the perimeter of the panel to make neat, finished edges.

step 4   (Shot 3) Countersink the nails with the nail set and fill in any nail holes, gaps and seams with wood filler. Let dry for 1 hour. Sand smooth the areas where you have applied wood filler. Seal the wood filler with primer and then touch up using the artist's brush and charcoal paint.

step 5   Mount the panel in position on the wall with screws.

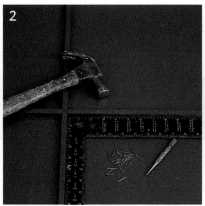
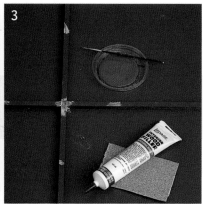

cottage
bedroom

The joys of a weekend playing at the cottage are surpassed only by tumbling into a country bed at night. It is the simplicity of country life that makes the decorating unique. I found all the furnishings for this tiny bedroom at the local country market. An old wrought-iron bed was freshened up with a coat of metal primer and two coats of white paint. Freestanding shutters painted a delicate blush pink diffuse the light and also add privacy. Crisp white linens and floral pillows contrast beautifully with the apple green walls. Traditionally, country colors tend to be darker tones of earthy greens, berry blues and rusty reds. The more contemporary country look is a shabby chic combination of pastels, off-whites, and comfortable secondhand finds that build a young, fresh, welcoming feeling.

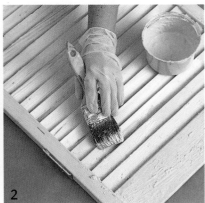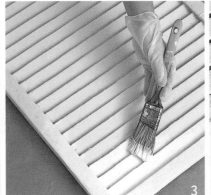

MATERIALS AND TOOLS

wood shutters or louvered doors

plaster of Paris

dusty pink latex paint, satin

mixing container

two 2″ paintbrushes

white latex paint, semi- or high-gloss

medium grit sandpaper

Shutters are traditionally attached to the walls, but they also make great screens that are both practical and decorative. Hinged together and with feet attached to the bottom of each shutter for balance, they can spread out in front of a window or be folded into a corner. (You could also use louver doors.) The wood shutters were first cleaned, then plaster of Paris was pretinted blush pink and painted over the entire surface. The trick is to do the worst paint job possible—leave globs of paint stuck in the corners and a lumpy uneven finish. White gloss paint goes over the dry plaster of Paris. Finally, I sanded the shutters to remove some of the white from the bumps and rough areas to reveal the pink, and sanded down to the bare wood in spots.

step 1　(*Shot 1*) Mix 1 cup of plaster of Paris with 1 cup of pink latex paint.

step 2　(*Shot 2*) Brush the mixture roughly onto the shutters, leaving some drips and thin and thick patches. Let dry overnight.

step 3　(*Shot 3*) Cover the pink with one coat of white gloss paint. Let dry for 4 hours.

step 4　(*Shot 4*) Sand over the surface to take the white paint off where the shutters are most roughly textured to reveal the pink underneath. Sand down further in some patches to reveal the original wood.

ebony &
ivory

Ebony is as dark and rich as bitter chocolate. The sleekness and durability of this spectacular wood have made it a popular choice for high-end furnishings. However, real ebony is scarce and therefore very expensive. My friend Andreas was decorating not only on a tight budget, but in a limited space. Although his bed fit snugly into an alcove, it looked rather squished. I fashioned this oversized headboard to look and feel like ebony with inlays of a lighter wood, but it is just plywood. There is little visible grain in the real wood, just a dark, deep patina that is very simple to re-create with paint. An etched mirror inscribed with Andreas' favorite Swedish nursery rhyme is centered on the wall at a height where the bed pillows will overlap the bottom of the frame. This is important as it gives the illusion that the oversized frame is a modern headboard. Etching fluid is permanent and toxic, so you must wear rubber gloves and eye protection and work in a well-ventilated room. Once the design on the mirror is complete, adhere the mirror to the wall with glue and then screw the ebony frame around the mirror. The results are smart and sexy.

Sov du lilla vide ung, än så är det vinter. Än så sova björk och ljung, ros och hyacinter. Än så är det långt till vår, innan rönn i blomma står. Sov du lilla vide, än så är det vinter.

ebony on a
plywood budget

EBONY FRAME

MATERIALS AND TOOLS

plywood sheets to cut for 4 sides of the frame (our vertical sides are 70" x 18", horizontal sides 34" × 18")

right-angle ruler

pencil

jigsaw

wood primer

roller and paint tray

yellow/beige, red/brown, chocolate brown and black latex paint, satin

fine sandpaper

two 3" coarse-bristle paintbrushes

1/8" low-tack painter's tape

acrylic varnish, satin

varnish brush or sponge roller

Because Andreas' bedroom is so small, we cut a square headboard frame to cover the width of the wall behind the bed. There is a small gap at the top of the wall. The vertical pieces run straight down the wall, and the horizontal pieces are cut shorter to fit in between. The mirror is also square and makes a smart contemporary focal point. There are two stages to the project: painting the ebony frame and etching the mirror. The etched mirror is glued to the wall first, and the ebony frame is installed around the mirror.

step 1   Measure and cut the 4 sides of the frame from the plywood. You will need two 70″ × 18″ strips and two 34″ × 18″ strips to make the square. (Since the horizontal pieces fit in between the long verticals, subtract twice the width of the board to get their length: 70″ − 36″ = 34″.)

step 2   Prime the plywood and apply 2 coats of yellow/beige paint, letting each coat dry and sanding lightly between coats. Let dry for 4 hours.

step 3   (Shot 1) Dip a paintbrush about 1″ into the red/brown and then the chocolate brown paint. Apply the paint in straight strokes running in the direction of the grain. Don't blend the two colors completely, and let some of the base coat peek through. Let dry for 4 hours.

step 4   (Shot 2) In the center of the two vertical sides of the frame, apply ten ⅛″ bands of tape 1½″ apart. Press down firmly. Dip the other paintbrush into the chocolate brown and then very lightly into the black and apply as in step 3. Go right over the ⅛″ tape.

step 5   (Shot 3) Let dry overnight, then carefully remove the tape.

step 6   Apply 2 coats of varnish and let dry.

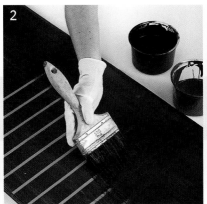
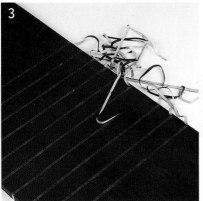

ETCHED MIRROR

MATERIALS AND TOOLS

mirror (ours is 34" square)
piece of text enlarged to desired size
graphite (carbon) paper
wide low-tack painter's tape
ruler
pencil
indelible marker
X-acto knife
rubber gloves
protective goggles
glass etching cream
container
sea sponge
bucket of water
rags
level
mirror glue
screws and plugs
wood filler
small (½") paint brush

step 1 (*Shot 1*) Tape the graphite paper to the back of the piece of text to be transferred. Stick strips of tape in straight lines across the mirror where you want the text to go. Use a ruler to make sure the writing will be straight. Center and position the graphite-backed text over the tape with the graphite side touching the tape. Trace the text onto the tape with a pencil.

step 2 (*Shot 2*) Remove the text piece from the tape and if the tracing isn't clear, go over the letters with a marker. Cut around the letters with the X-acto knife and remove all the tape around the letters, leaving behind only the words in tape on the mirror.

step 3 (*Shot 3*) Put on the gloves and goggles. Pour some etching cream into a container. Apply the cream all over the mirror with the sea sponge. The sponge will make the etching slightly uneven and will give the mirror an antiqued look.

step 4 Let the cream sit on the mirror for 3 to 10 minutes depending on the directions printed on the etching cream box. With hands and eyes still protected, rinse off the etching cream with the rag and water and dry the mirror.

step 5 (*Shot 4*) Remove all the tape letters and wash and dry the mirror again.

step 6 Apply mirror glue to the back of the mirror and adhere it in position on the wall. Use the level to make sure it is straight. The frame's sides are butted up against the mirror and screwed onto the wall. Countersink the screws, fill the holes with wood filler and let dry. Sand smooth and then touch up using the small brush and some dark brown paint.

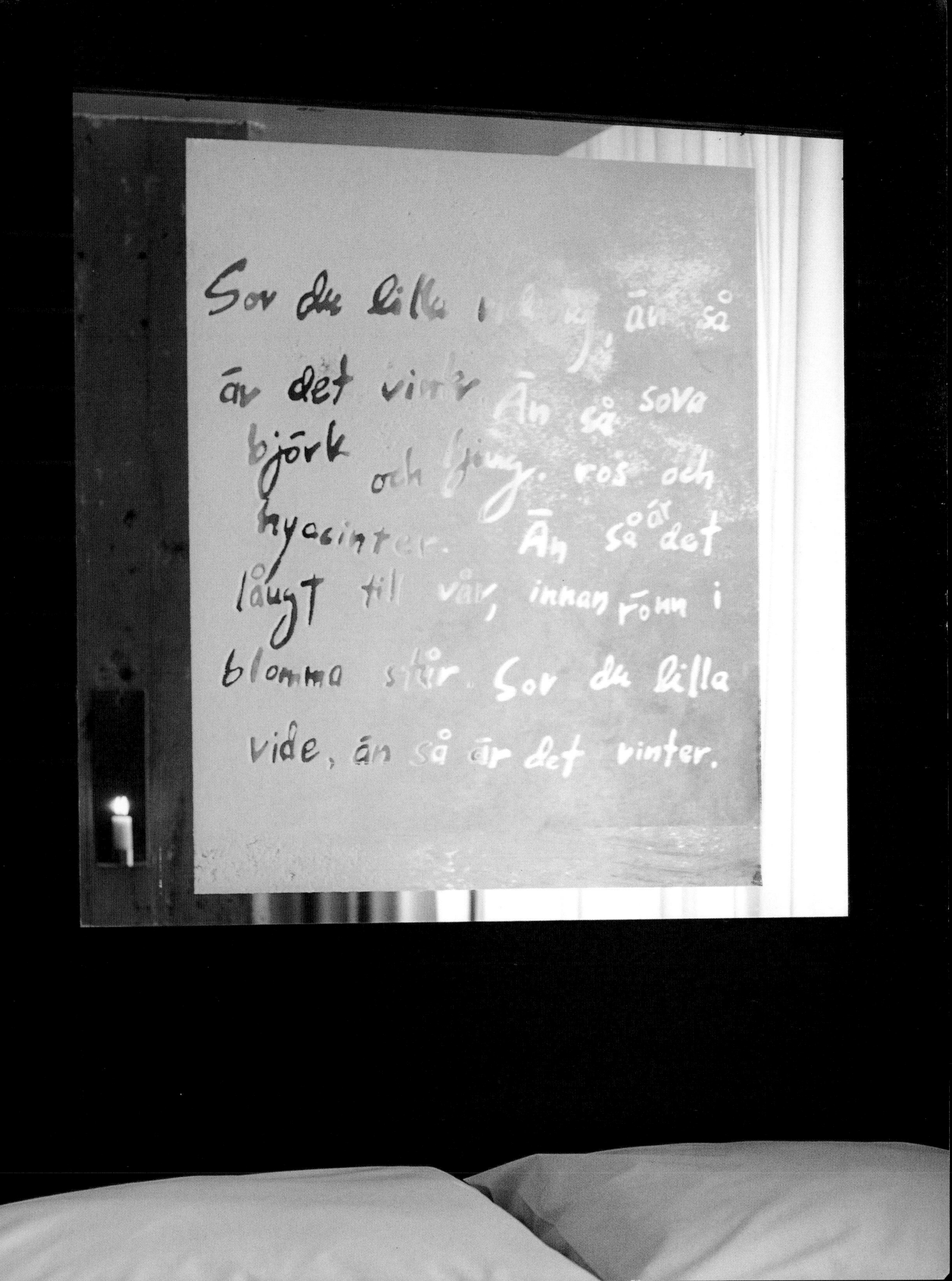
Sov du lilla
än så
är det
Än så sova
björk och ljung. ros och
hyacinter. Än så är det
långt till vår, innan rönn i
blomma står. Sov du lilla
vide, än så är det vinter.

resources

Debbie Travis Specialty Collection—a line of specialty products such as glaze, suede paint, stone finish stucco, and more for the contemporary, elegant interior. Available through the Painted House website, www.painted-house.com, or by calling 1-800-932-3446.

elements of the bedroom

bedding on page 14
Toile sur Rendezvous
Tel: (514) 486-2424
info@linensbyappointment.com

bedding on page 18
MATTEO
Tel: (213) 617-2813
1-888-MATTEO-1
Fax: (213) 617-2816
www.matteohome.com
info@matteohome.com

allergy control (page 20)

BioShield Paints—Environmentally safe, natural paints
United States
Tel: (800) 621-2591
Fax: (505) 438-0199
International
Tel: (505) 438-3448
Fax: (505) 438-0199
www.bioshieldpaint.com
edesignco@aol.com

hypoallergenic bedding and natural products
Terra Verde
Tel: (212) 925-4533
Fax: (212) 925-4540
www.terraverde.com

cork floor distributor (page 26)
Torlys—Leaders in specialty flooring
Tel: (905) 612-8772
Toll Free: (800) 461-2573
Fax: (905) 612-9049
www.torlys.com
postmaster@torlys.com

inspiration from afar
Jake's, Jamaica
Tel: (800) 330-8272
www.jakescottages.com
Palazzo Terranova, Perugia, Italy
Tel: +39 075 857 0083
www.palazzoterranova.com
Charlton House, Somerset, England
Tel: 01749 342008
www.charltonhouse.com
The W Hotel, New York, New York, U.S.A
Tel: (212) 755-1200
www.starwood.com/whotels
The Kent, Miami, Florida, U.S.A.
Tel: (800) OUTPOST
www.islandoutpost.com/Kent/
Lake Placid Lodge, Lake Placid, New York, U.S.A.
Tel: (877) 523-2700
www.lakeplacidlodge.com
The Hotel Place D'Armes, Montreal, Quebec, Canada
Tel: (888) 450-1887
www.hotelplacedarmes.com